Teaching the Youngest Writers:
A Practical Guide

by
Marcia S. Freeman

For Primary-grade Teachers

Teaching The Youngest Writers: A Practical Guide
© copyright 1998 Marcia S. Freeman

Marcia S. Freeman is a writer and consultant specializing in the practical aspects of creating and managing a classroom writing community. She is the author of *Building a Writing Community: A Practical Guide* and *Listen to This: Developing an Ear for Expository*. Ms. Freeman appreciates comments and suggestions. Please write or e-mail her in care of the publisher.

Editor: *Candace Nelson*
Cover design: *David Dishman*
Book design: *Billie J. Hermansen*

Freeman, Marcia S. (Marcia Sheehan), 1937-
    Teaching the youngest writers : a practical guide / by Marcia S. Freeman.
        p.   cm.
    "For primary grade teachers."
    Includes bibliographical references (p.   ) and index.
    1. English language--Composition and exercises--Study and teaching (Primary)--United States--Handbooks, manuals, etc.   I. Title.
LB1529.U5F74   1998
372.62'3--DC21
                                                  98-15274
                                                      CIP

Maupin House Publishing, Inc.
PO Box 90148
Gainesville, FL 32607-0148
1-800-524-0634
jgraddy@maupinhouse.com

Dedication

In loving memory of my mother, Marion Frazer.

Table of Contents

Section Four: Evaluation, Parent Education, Questions/Answers

Foreword

More and more states are assessing writing in the intermediate grades using a prompted narrative or essay. Fourth-grade teachers know they alone can not prepare students for such an assessment test. School administrators and faculties are looking critically at their school-wide writing programs. They are asking: How early can we start writing instruction and how should we proceed?

We can start writing instruction in kindergarten. We can start on the first day of school, establishing the expectation that youngsters will learn to read and write. We don't need to wait until children know all their letters, know all their sound-to-symbol relationships, know how to spell all the words they want to use. We don't need to wait until children can read. Young children are *writers* as soon as they draw or put a symbol on paper and tell us what it says. We should call them writers and treat them as writers from that moment on.

If we start in the earliest grades teaching print principles, expository and narrative techniques, composing and convention skills, and providing for lots of practice, we can help children become good writers. We know this because many primary teachers create successful writing communities in which their students achieve a high degree of elaboration — writing several sentences to develop an idea or topic — and a strong sense of authorship.

These teachers do it by making writing instruction a top priority in their schedule. They conduct daily writing workshops; they encourage young writers to talk, draw, write, and share their work; they teach writing skills and techniques.

They have learned empirically that children who apply their emerging phonetic skills to their writing learn to read faster than children who do not. They have discovered empirically that children's spelling evolves from experimental and temporary spelling to conventional spelling. They know that children revise and edit their work as a natural result of sharing it and publishing it in a community of writers.

When children from these successful writing communities enter third grade, their teachers are astounded by their use and knowledge of the writing process: *Where shall we meet for Author's Chair?; I need a peer conference; Will you read my piece for specificity?* They are amazed by their knowledge of genre: *Kelly's narrative has no focus; That's a nice hook; I like question hooks; Look how I used a simile.*

This book describes the attributes of an active community of the youngest writers and how to create such a community. It is about teaching young writers the elements of writing, the nature of written text, and the writing process. It describes classroom-tested practices, writing-process mechanisms, management techniques, and appropriate lessons that successful teachers use to help children become fluent writers.

Introduction

The Youngest Writers

The youngest writers are emergent writers who, initially, are not be able to read today what they wrote yesterday. Their first writing does not contain enough recognizable symbols for them to reconstruct the words they used to tell what they know or to express their ideas and feelings. These writers share a number of other attributes as well.

- They are becoming aware of written symbols and are learning the relationship between the sounds of their language and the symbols that represent those sounds. They are learning to draw those symbols. They are experimenting with them. *Does an upside down or backward b work?*

- They are learning printed-text principles. *Can I write around the edge of the page? Can I start on the right?*

- They write about themselves. They know this topic best.

- They love to tell what they know, whether it is appropriate or not. Their natural mode of writing is **informational expository**: *I love my dog; This is me; I saw a fish.* What they communicate is information that is important to them. They communicate it first through oral language and drawings.

- They do not write narratives (stories) to start. They do not write stories until we have read so many stories to them that they think this is the important mode so they abandon their natural inclination to write informational expository.

- They do not consciously organize their writing. They present information in the order they think of it or the order of its importance to them.

- They do not capitalize the first word of their writing. They are learning the alphabet in its two forms: uppercase and lowercase, and they cannot use it with any consistency.

In sum, they are *learning* to write. And, however meager their skills, as soon as they see that marks on a paper can convey a message, they *are* writers. It is crucial that we regard them and treat them as such.

We can encourage and help children use their sound-to-symbol awareness, their drawings, their marks, single letters, and groups of letters to satisfy their natural urge to communicate ideas and express their feelings. We can teach them the skills they will need to record what they see, what they feel, what they hear, and what they know.

The Writing Process

The writing process is how we translate ideas into written text. It starts with an idea and the need to develop it, communicate it to an audience, and preserve it. *Every* writer, at every age and every stage of development and proficiency, goes through this process.

Writers begin the process by gathering thoughts and information, talking about the subject, and planning their presentation. Next, they write. Then they share the text with someone to get a response. They revise the text until it is clear and interesting. Finally, they polish it for presentation, and they publish. This is not a linear process, for writers must often go back to rethink, re-plan, and reconstruct parts of the text that failed to convey their information and ideas.

In this book I describe each writing-process stage *as it applies to emergent and early developing writers.* Take revision, for example: When emergent writers tell or read their pieces, they will add to the *text*, ad-libbing as they take another look at their drawings. When they read to a peer or the teacher they often say, *"Oh, I forgot..."* and tell more about their pictures. If you talk to them about their drawing/writing, they might go back and **add another element** to their drawings, or **add another label** to the pictures. They might **add another mark or letter** below the picture. They may **add another word or sentence** to their message. All these activities represent revision at the emergent-writing level.

A Curriculum of Writing Content

An effective curriculum must provide the information and techniques young writers need to learn how to write. Writing, as does science, social studies, music, math, and art, includes a body of knowledge, a *content*. That content consists of expository and narrative genre characteristics, composing and literary skills, and writing conventions. It is taught through the use of the writing process.

Lessons

The lessons and demonstrations in this book are based on the thesis that **need** drives the acquisition of skills. We learn a skill best when we need that skill and therefore have the incentive to learn it. We understand why we are learning and we fully engage in the learning process.

Consider, for example, how you learned to use a computer. Did you read the entire manual, memorizing how to do a mail merge when you were interested only in revising your recipes? Apply the same principle to your writing program. For example:

- Introduce finger spaces when young writers are using strings of scribbles or letters for a sentence.
- Teach young writers to use comparisons when they want to describe something.
- Teach them end punctuation when they are writing more than one sentence.

Plan your lessons to fit their needs.

Target Skills

Young writers learn by imitating. Take advantage of this by modeling all the writing techniques you can. In this book, I refer to them as **Target Skills**. (Read Chapter 11 before you plan your writing-instruction program.) Target skills are the subjects of lessons; they are the techniques children practice; they are the skills that you call for in a piece; they are the skills children identify in peer conferences; they are the skills you look for in children's writing. Their use is proof that young writers are making progress.

You will find many places in this book where I have left spaces for you to create your own lesson models. Take the time to write and draw them. You will be more effective using your own models than using mine. Creating them will reinforce your understanding of the skill and improve your own writing as well.

Tab the pages so you can find your models quickly when you need them in writing workshop. After you have used some of them successfully, you will probably want to develop them further and keep them in a separate notebook.

Concrete Aids

You will notice as you read this book that I use many objects and manipulative aids in the models and lessons. Primary-grade students are in the concrete-operational stage of mental development. (See Piaget, in your Educational Psychology notes.) Dealing with real objects — things they can handle — will greatly facilitate their learning. When you plan your lessons, look for ways to incorporate an object — a tool, a sticker, a color, a shape, etc.

Using This Book: Symbols

In each chapter, I describe specific models, lessons, and procedures that have been tested in classrooms like yours. Each one works because it answers the needs of young writers.

It contributes to the structure or workings of the classroom writing community, or it provides writing-craft information.

These models, lessons, and procedures are coded to show you where they fit in your daily writing workshop.

Getting Started   Field Notes

Writing   Sharing

Professional Reading

As teachers, we need to cultivate a continuing professional habit of reading books about writing. Our ability to teach the craft is limited by our knowledge of it. Start with books written for children. They contain essential information and will help you focus on specific areas to research at more advanced levels. See Bibliography for books about the writing craft.

A Writing Community in the Primary Grades

Children go through distinct stages of development as they learn to write. These stages are characterized by common, observable writing behavior. Children's writing demonstrates the concepts and principles they understand about written text.

Marie Clay, in *What Did I Write*, Portsmouth, NH: Heinemann, 1975, describes print principles and concepts.

Print Principles and Concepts

- Sign Concept: child realizes that a symbol carries a message.
- Message Concept: child realizes that a spoken message can be written down.
- Copying Principle: child traces and copies in an attempt to "write."
- Flexibility Principle: child experiments with letters — reverses, writes upside down — and discovers conventionality of letter symbols.
- Inventorying Principle: child lists what he knows — letters, words, phrases, etc.
- Recurring Principle: child repetitively uses groups of words for competence and confidence: *I like... I have a...*
- Directional Principle: child learns text goes left to right and top to bottom of page, it wraps and continues on next page, top left again.
- Ordering Principle: child groups and sorts symbols, sounds, and word patterns.
- Space Principle: child moves from single words and labeling to words with finger spaces. (Hearing separate words in spoken language is difficult, and children vary in their ability to do so.)
- Generating Principle: child starts to create his own text from known elements.

Emergent and Early-developing Writing Stages

Young writers can be described in terms of the writing behavior they exhibit. Numbers or descriptive stage-labels create a helpful reference system for diagnosing, planning instruction, and reporting progress.

The first three stages describe children who have not made the sound-to-symbol connection, but are beginning to understand that marks on a paper convey a message.

Stage One, Picture Writer: Communicates by drawing or making random marks, may not be able to tell about picture or marks. (No understanding that symbols convey a message.)

Stage Two, Verbal Informer: Chooses own topic. Tells about picture. Drawing contains few details. May make random symbols. Some letters and numbers show great variation of form and have no relation to sound.

Stage Three, Letter Copier: Chooses own topic. May draw or cut and paste pictures. Tells about picture. Labels drawings with symbols or letters, and may write strings of letters (often those of own name) with no sound-to-symbol relation. Copies environmental print and text from books.

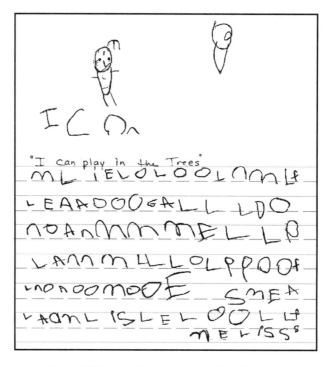

The next two stages describe children who are learning that letters represent language sounds and that words and text convey meaning.

Stage Four, Labeler: Chooses own topic. Drawing is more detailed. Labels the important parts of the drawing with starting letter of word and tells about drawing with details integrated. Writes strings of consonants with some sound-to-symbol relationship. Shows left-to-right movement of writing.

Stage Five, Inventory Taker/Sound Maker: Chooses own topic. Tells about picture. Writes with a letter-to-word correspondence (b is boy, d is dog), some words consisting of first and last consonants. Begins to write inventories of known letters, words, or phrases. MLMMMMMLLLLL. Or, *I love my d. I love my k. I love my mom.*

The final stages describe children who understand which letters represent which language sounds, and that words and text follow a standard form.

Stage Six, Sentence Maker: Chooses own topic. More emphasis on writing than drawing. Begins to use finger spaces. Generates strings of words using first and last consonant, some medial vowels, words learned by rote. May wrap text. Begins to put period at end of writing.

Stage Seven, Information Communicator/Story Maker: Chooses own topic. Emphasis mainly on writing; drawing often follows writing. More consistency in letter form (case), uses blends, digraphs, medial vowels. Writes high frequency words. Writes from left to right. Writes more than one sentence about an idea or topic.

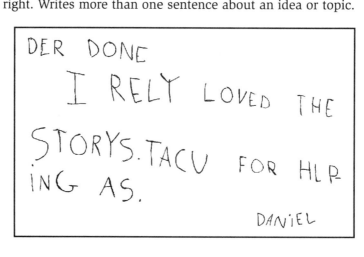

Cautionary Notes:

1. Children may simultaneously exhibit characteristics of two or more stages, reflecting different levels of print concepts and sound-to-symbol understanding.

2. Do not attach a grade to a stage during the emergent writer's development. That would be like grading babies for their walking skill. *Sorry, you are only sitting by yourself; you get an F in walking. And you, you are just crawling, so you get a D.* Note students' progress through the stages by recording the date when a characteristic of a stage first appears in their writing.

The Teacher's Task: Model, Teach Lessons, and Provide Time for Practice

Your job as a primary-grade teacher is to help young writers progress through the writing stages. You must model writing to demonstrate print principles. You must show children how to choose topics and use the writing process. You must teach your young writers the content of writing — the genre characteristics, composing and literary skills, and writing conventions. Throughout the entire book, you will find the models and techniques children need in order to make this progress

By the time young writers reach Stages Five, Six, and Seven, they are able to read their writing the day after they wrote it. At this point they are *developing writers*. Now they need lessons designed to improve the quality of their writing and ample time to practice. Writing is a developmental process, a craft, and as such, **requires a great deal of practice**. Young writers have to write often, with objective target skills, before they can write well.

Successful Writing Communities

Teachers who create successful writing communities value what children have to say and believe that children can and will write. They model strategies for solving the puzzle of writing. They are willing to relinquish control of topic choice — giving students ownership of their writing. They provide the time, tools, structure, audience, lessons, and resources for children to become independent writers. These teachers create a supportive and secure environment wherein young writers are willing to take risks.

To create a successful classroom writing community you will need to:

- schedule a consistent and sufficient block of time for daily writing,
- create an environment conducive to writing,
- rehearse writing-workshop procedures involving materials, movement, and writing-process mechanisms,
- use writers' vocabulary,
- create written models to demonstrate printed-text principles and target skills,
- teach target-skill lessons about the expository and narrative genre, composing skills, and conventions,
- create evaluation techniques for both you and your writers to use,
- keep records and build student writing portfolios,
- teach parents about your writing program.

*   *   *

Teaching the Youngest Writers **is all about how to do these things.**

Section One: Daily Writing Workshop

Chapter 1
A Classroom that Promotes Writing

Establishing Goals

Before you set up your room in preparation for a new year and a new crop of young writers, establish your goals. Here are some achievements you can reasonably expect from primary children *if you conduct a daily writing workshop, and teach children writing information and techniques.*

Kindergarten teachers should expect most students, by the end of the year, to:

- write in complete sentences, using a variety of styles including strings of consonants that represent a word, or strings of words consisting of starting and ending consonants, with or without median vowels, with finger spaces between *words*, and conventional spelling for some common sight-words
- form most of the upper- and lower-case letters, though using them interchangeably
- choose a topic independently
- know how to compliment another writer
- share their writing with the class or a peer
- revise by adding color or an element or label to a drawing, or by adding more letters to the message
- hear the difference between an information piece and a story
- edit each other's papers for the author's name, a title, and a period at the end of all the writing
- select best work based on personal or class criteria (See Chapter 16),
- hand-publish (with adult help) a collection of best work or contribute one page to a class book

First-grade teachers should expect most students, by the end of the year, to:

- form all upper- and lower-case letters, and use them with some consistency
- write in complete sentences
- choose a topic independently
- write several sentences on one topic in the personal expository and personal narrative genres
- use a combination of transitional or temporary spelling and, increasingly, conventional spelling for common sight words
- share their writing with a peer or the class
- identify the use of a target skill in another writer's piece
- know how to compliment and ask questions of another writer
- revise by adding words and sentences
- use a small variety of *hooks* to start their information pieces (see Chapter 13)
- use a variety of *attributes* and *comparisons* in description
- edit each other's papers for a capital letter for I, first word of the piece, and first word of a sentence; a period at the end of a sentence and at the end of the entire piece

- select best work for their portfolios based on personal or class criteria for good writing, and
- hand-publish two pieces

(See Appendix for Grade Two goals.)

These writing-instruction goals should complement your reading-instruction goals. They both rest on a foundation of language facility. Think of reading and writing as extensions of listening and talking that take us from the fleeting to the enduring.

Achieving These Goals

Your first big step — one that teachers who build communities of the youngest writers will tell you is a huge one — is to absolutely expect your students to write. Act on that premise. In the beginning, treat them as writers, call them writers, make them believe they are writers. Have faith: *Build it and they will come.*

As your students begin the exciting quest of solving the puzzle of printed text, you and they will need to develop specific attitudes and accept certain responsibilities. These are:

Attitudes

- Writing is important.
- We continually improve our writing.
- We share our knowledge of the writing craft with one another.
- Our writing belongs to us.

Your responsibilities

- Conduct a daily writing workshop.
- Provide lessons and the time to practice the skills you teach.
- Model everything: procedures, mechanics of writing, the nature of text, writing techniques, etc.
- Leave control of the topic (content) to the writer.
- Help young writers publish.

Student's responsibilities

- Write about things you know.
- Try to use target skills.
- Share your writing with peers.
- Phrase your comments and questions in a polite manner.
- Revise by using a target skill.
- Help as an editor.
- Publish your best writing.

Setting up Your Room

The physical environment of your room must support your daily writing workshop. Young writers need a place to write, to talk and conference, to meet with you in a group for lessons and sharing, and to store their writing. Here are some of the things that will help you build a writing community in your classroom:

- **a place for children to talk, listen, and write** — Tables or paired desks work well. The room should be arranged so there are areas for quiet work and areas where young writers may interact with each other and you.

  Talking as they draw is the prewriting activity of choice for most young writers. (If you watch them, you will see they do not even require that their partners listen.) Sharing their writing also encourages children to help each other. When your writing community is underway, you will not be able to interact with every child each session. Students-helping-students will be an integral part of your daily writing workshop.

- **a gathering place in front of an easel** — Make it large enough to seat the whole class comfortably, with room for students to move without bumping into a classmate.

- **a special chair** — a rocking chair, director's chair, or such, labeled **Author's Chair** — Place the chair near the easel and your classroom library.

Author's Chair

- **a place to spread a large strip of paper** during writing workshop — A section of uncarpeted floor, a long table, or wall space will do fine. (See Help Strip on page 22.)

- **a book display** — A tiered bookcase shows the front of most of the books, as do large plastic tubs or baskets. Many teachers label the tubs or displays by author, genre, or theme. Do not put all your books out at the start of the year. Rotate collections so that children discover new books, and rediscover old favorites at later times during the year. Make sure you have enough books displayed — at least one for each child — at any one time.

- **wall surfaces for word banks** — A movable bulletin board, the back of a bookcase, a side wall, the sides of filing cabinets, and the area under the blackboard all work. They should be no higher than the children can reach. Young writers will need to take word cards to their writing place and put them back again. Use tacky-putty, clothespins on wires or twine, or pockets on fabric boards.

  You can make a quick chart from a plastic hanger with a long strip of unlined paper stapled to the cross bar. Hang it on a door knob, from furniture, or from wires and strings attached to the ceiling.

- Start the wall word bank with some basic sight words, i.e., the Dolch Primary list. Then add words that the children frequently request. (See Word Banks on page 68.)

- **a storage place for children's writing** — Use a shelf for student-writing folders stored in caddies (laundry baskets, tubs, crates), large legal-size portfolios, or stackable, corrugated cardboard pizza boxes (donated through a school-business partnership).

  Storing student writing is a crucial aspect to your emergent writing community. **Children must keep a body of writing in school**. Because young students are not good at keeping track of their papers, the storage system must be chaos proof.

Materials

Provide your young writers with a large variety of tools and concrete materials to encourage their writing. Among these are:

- **writing tools of all sorts** — markers, crayons, pencils, chalk, and sponges or paintbrushes for water-writing on blackboards and sidewalks

  Young children are notorious for losing their pencils. They break the points so they can go to the pencil sharpener. They use them for digging on the playground. They can think of a dozen uses for them that the manufacturer never dreamed possible.

  Keep a supply of pencils in a canister on your desk. Know that you are going to be supplying many of your children with pencils all year. It would be lovely if they were responsible enough to remember to have a pencil each day, but you know that is not how five-, six-, and seven-year-olds operate.

Find a sensible way to have pencils ready for writing workshop. Ask an older student to make that a personal, daily school job. Find a reliable supply: parents, small businesses, retirees, garage sales.

- **writing surfaces of all sorts** — sections of sidewalks for water-writing (Tell your custodial staff of your plans.), individual or small whiteboards, individual slates, green- or bluebar accounting paper (11" by 14" version, from an office-supply store), unlined paper (recycled copy paper), large newsprint, etc. Some teachers give emergent writers a stapled folio of five to ten unlined sheets covered with construction paper for several days of writing. Stamp the date on the folio. A series of folios will reflect a child's progress.

  Business partners can supply you with used copier paper for drawing and writing. (Publish, though, on new paper.) Keep the recycled paper in a box where children can get it on their own. Encourage conservation, but remember that paper is what writers need and use. We cannot afford to be stingy when it comes to paper for our young writers.

- **spiral-bound or composition notebooks** for first graders to use for daily writing or homework journaling

- **green- or bluebar** computer accounting paper (not the carbon-paper type) has large bi-colored lines. Young writers love this paper as their first lined paper. They can write on either the white or the colored line, leaving room for additive revision on the other. The paper is unlined on the back for drawing. Children can erase at will, the paper holds up well. It comes in both 8 1/2" by 11", and a great primary paper size, 11" by 14". This larger size folds to form an instant book, the unlined back of the paper becoming the cover.

  Place 5-10 sheets of greenbar paper in an opened file folder. Staple the sheets to the left hand edge of the folder. Fold the papers in half and close the folder for easy storage.

- **sentence-strips paper** — 2" by 11" trimmings of heavy-weight paper are usually available free from a commercial print shop. The strips are excellent for list making, sentence dictation, and fact gathering.

- **a picture collection** — magazine pictures with kid-appeal cut from *National Geographic, Ranger Rick, Sports Illustrated*, the local newspaper, pet and hobby magazines, etc., and a collection of art prints. Ask for magazines at dentist's and doctor's offices, school and public libraries. Ask friends and relatives to clip and send you pictures.

  Some teachers set up file folders in milk crates for children to access the collection: animals, children and people in action, inside places, outside places, vehicles, sports, etc. Label and arrange the files in alphabetical order.

- **ABC strips** taped to tables and desk tops, or laminated, 8" by 11" card-stock ABC charts for each child to keep in his writing folder, or for storage in a writing center

  The traditional handwriting ABC strips should not be placed high on the wall over the blackboard. It is visually difficult for children to use these as models for the letters they need as they write. Attach a set of them below the blackboard or at the children's eye-level.

- **ABC letter patterns, clay, finger paints, and small paint brushes for water-writing** are all useful manipulative tools to help emergent writers practice forming letters. The ABC letter patterns — cardboard or wooden — allow children to trace the straight and curved lines of each letter in the correct sequence when they print the alphabet. These patterns are large, and children with underdeveloped fine-motor skills need them. (See Bibliography for sources.)

- **self-sticking labels** — Include small, colored, die-cut file labels or smiley-face labels in your budget or ask stores or parents to donate them. Young writers will use them for compliments and questions in peer conferences. (See Chapter 7 for their use in peer conferences and Author's Chair.)

  Larger white labels or scraps of labeling paper are useful to repair tears in children's papers, or to cover an erasure hole so a child can write over it.

- **rolls of butcher paper**, doctors' examining-table paper, shelf paper, backs of rolled wallpaper — These will be used for the Help Strip, a procedure described in Chapter 4.

- **clipboards** — Most school districts will provide these upon request.

- **a collection of Big Books** (easel-sized children's books) — All genres should be represented: informational, stories, poetry. All kinds of text should be available: repetitious, patterned, predictable, rhyming, with or without dialogue, etc.

- **each child's name on a 4" by 11" laminated card**, connected by a large ring through a hole in the left-hand end of each card — Take attendance with the whole class standing in a circle. A child whose turn it is will take attendance saying, "*Good morning, Alex. Good morning, Jessica,*" as he flips each card over.

- **a large supply of key rings**, clothes pins, or shower-curtain rings to clip word cards or papers together

- **blank transparency film** and an overhead projector

Optional:

- **two to six Writer's Kits** — small pieces of luggage or lunch packs filled with writing tools, paper, folded-paper booklets, ink stamps, stencils, scissors, clips, hole puncher, glue — all the things a child and adult can use to make a book together. You may want to have a limited number to start, making it a special thing for a young writer to take one home. Later, all your writers may want to take one home. If you have five or six, children can use them on a rotational basis.

- **a class mascot** — a plastic or stuffed animal labeled with your classroom number and school name

- **A microphone for Author's Chair is** a great optional item. Many teachers use an inexpensive microphone jacked into a portable tape deck.

  If you cannot arrange for some form of electronic amplification for Author's Chair, be sure to place the chair in the corner of a room. The surrounding walls will act as a megaphone, and children's voices will carry a bit farther than if the chair were placed in front of a flat wall.

Model Everything

Model everything. That's it — the key to a successful primary writing community.

Teachers of active writing communities take the time to model and periodically re-model everything: workshop procedures, writing-process components, writing mechanics, composing and literary skills, organization schemes, genre characteristics, self-evaluation.

Their models include aural, oral, visual, and kinesthetic features to accommodate the learning modes of all their students.

To present models smoothly, you need to think them through, rehearse them, and prepare the requisite materials. I have included space throughout the book for you to create models. Perfect the techniques you will need to teach emergent writers. Remember, writing is a craft, and children learn it best by imitation

When you use students in your models, of course, use a *plant*. A plant is a pre-arranged person in the audience who, for example, feeds the politician the perfect question or who the magician calls on as a "random volunteer." For your modeling, choose children for the volume of their voices, their ability to articulate, or the content of their writing.

Tab the model and lesson pages, draw and write your own models. Script them and practice them. They are the basis, the very core, of your writing program.

Some examples of what to model:

- how to choose a topic
- how to make letters
- in what direction print text is written
- how to get help
- how to peer conference
- how to use target skills
- how to write a hook
- how to revise by adding another label
- how to end a personal narrative (when children start to order events in sequence)

You will find some models in this book appropriate for kindergarten children and others for first and second graders. Since most primary classes contain a range of writing levels, from Stage-One emergent writers to developing writers, the models will be previews for some, reviews for others, and right on target for the rest.

Writers' Vocabulary

Young students should be introduced to writers' vocabulary as soon as you start daily writing workshop. They like big words, and they like to be treated as writers.

Manuscript talk

The first thing you will want to do is refer to students' writing as *your writing*, or *your picture writing*, or *your piece*. Do not call their writing, *your story*, unless it is a story.

> A simple explanation of the difference between narrative, story, and expository writing is: narrative is a chronological record of events (time passes) and expository is everything else. Expository is information, explanation, opinion, and persuasion.

If we call everything a *story*, we are placing undue emphasis on narrative and fiction. During a lifetime, almost everything almost everyone writes is expository in nature. In fact, almost all emergent writers' early works are expository in nature: Scribble — *That's me and my cat*; TDZB — *The dog is big*; I lv mi mm — *I love my mom*. The best approach is to call all writing by its genre or form name — *invitation, letter, information, piece, story, etc.*

Book talk

When you read to your class, introduce them to the vocabulary of books and informational articles: *title, author, illustrator, title page, table of contents, caption, chart, photograph, character, setting, plot, dialogue, finger spaces, quotation marks, capital letters.* Encourage young writers to use these terms when they talk to you about their reading and writing.

Writing-process talk

Use writing-process terms such as *prewrite, plan, writing, manuscript, peer conference, conference, Author's Chair, compliment, revise, edit, publish.* I shy away from using the term *sloppy copy* for *draft* because children, so literal, often think the writing *must* be sloppy. Rough drafts need to be as readable as possible, particularly for the young authors themselves.

Writing-instruction talk

During lessons, use the vocabulary of genre, composition and literary techniques, and conventions: *target skill, alliteration, simile, hook, description, details, character, setting, rhyme, dialogue, compare, caret, verbs, nouns, setbacks, specificity, comma, period, capital, exclamation mark, question mark, etc.*

Of course, this vocabulary might pop up in the strangest fashion. In a second-grade class I visit, the children were working on specificity — using specific nouns instead of general ones: *I went to K Mart*, not, *I went to the store.* A child wrote in her whale report: *Whales live in the Spacific Ocean.*

Words are the tools we need to communicate. If we are to talk to children as writers, we need to use a writer's vocabulary.

Chapter 2
Daily Writing Workshop: Getting Started

When children anticipate writing every day, they prewrite and rehearse on the school bus, on the playground, in the lunchroom, in class, and at home. Parents should be encouraged to ask their child each morning, "What will you write about today?"

The Same Time Every Day

Daily writing workshop should be at the same time each day. Young students thrive on structure and stability.

The best time for daily writing workshop in the primary grades is during the morning language arts block. Language arts education occurs all day long in the primary grades. Most teachers, however, schedule a block of formal language arts training that may consist of a progression such as Show and Tell; phonics or letter work; reading aloud to students with a lesson about printed text or reading comprehension, and writing time for all the children. (Do read aloud to your students at other times during the day just for the sheer joy of it — no analysis, no stopping for discussion.)

Any activities that require children to sit and listen (e.g., Show and Tell, choral reading, reading aloud, or a writing lesson at the board or easel), need to be separated by some physical activity. This might include moving to a different place to draw and talk, singing, snacking, or stretching and marching to music.

You will need 45 minutes for the writing part of your language arts block. Do not begrudge devoting this amount of time to daily writing workshop. The time will be used efficiently because writing workshop incorporates talking, listening, reading, and writing throughout the session. And, we know that children who learn to write early, read early.

Getting Started

The First Day of School

On the first day of school, set up an easel or whiteboard and some markers by the door and ask students to sign in. Parents may help their kindergarten children make a mark, write their name, or do whatever they can do. From the start, your students will know that writing is expected and important in their class.

Additionally, on the first day of school when you are showing children around the room, gather them in front of an easel labeled *Class Meeting Place*. Place your *Author's Chair* beside it.
Put an appealing Big Book, an art print, or a sample of student writing from a previous year on the easel. Tell the children that you will all meet here each day. Point to the label and say the words. Have them repeat them with you: *This is the Author's Chair*. Point to the gathering place where they are standing or sitting, and have them repeat: *This is the class meeting place.*

The First Writing Workshop

In kindergarten, you might postpone the first writing workshop for a day or two, until the children settle into your classroom routines. During those days, however, make paper and writing tools freely available.

The following description of the first two days will give you an idea of how to get started. Your daily writing workshop will consist of three parts: a starting activity, the writing time, and the sharing time. In the next chapter, Conducting The Daily Writing Workshop, I describe daily writing workshop in detail: how to start, what the children are doing, what you are doing, how to end it. The remainder of the book deals with what to teach and how to do it.

The starting activity

In your scheduled writing time on the first day, gather your class to the easel and read to them. For this first oral reading choose an informational Big Book. Select one that is about something familiar to the children: animals, food, child activity, or such. Select one that is short, has huge text, is photo-illustrated, and has repetitive text. Invite the children to chorus with you as you read. When you are finished, invite them to tell what they liked best. Then say, *Didn't that author write a wonderful book?*

Point out that the author told us what she knows about the subject of the book. For example, *This author knows a lot about animals and their babies.* Now ask the children, *What do you know about? Do you know about cats or dogs, pizza or popcorn, fish or frogs?* Listen to several children tell what they know. Say, *I hope you'll tell us what you know now as we write.*

Ask everyone to stand and stretch. Re-seat them and model drawing/writing for them at the easel. Draw/write your own personal information piece on a large sheet of newsprint at the easel or on the chalk board.

For example: Draw a basic scene with just one or two elements. Talk as you work. *I'm going to tell you about my dog. He loves to run. This is him running. He runs in our yard.* Label the dog, D. Say, *That's my dog. D for dog.* Write two short sentences under the picture. Be sure the second sentence relates to the first. *My dog loves to run. He goes fast.* Read it aloud one more time.

If children say, *I can't write*, or, *I can't read*, assure them that they can draw and tell what they know.

Your Model For the First Day of Writing Workshop: Draw, label one or two elements, and write two sentences here for your first writing-workshop model. Be sure the second sentence relates to the first. This models cohesive writing. (See Single Sentence Syndrome, page 16.) Tab the page so you can find it quickly.

Writing time

Now give each child a sheet of unlined paper. I use unlined paper during the first weeks in both kindergarten and first grade until the students are comfortable with daily writing-workshop procedures. I have found that if I introduce traditional primary lined paper, its format — just two lines — tends to make children concentrate on convention rather than on their thoughts and makes them think one line of writing is required. (Large 11" by 14" greenbar paper does not seem to result in this inhibition.

Invite your students to write whatever they choose. *Tell us what you know.* Tell students they are to write at their tables or desks. Give them time to find a partner. Tell them they may talk softly to each other as they work on their drawing and writing. Demonstrate talking softly. I call it **murmur voices**. Some teachers have children rate their talking noise levels from one to three: one for partner talking, two for responding to the teacher, and three, *your playground voice,* for reciting to the whole class.

What You Will Do

You will act as if writing were no big deal; everyone can *write*. This means you are going to accept all your students' attempts at writing. In kindergarten and first grade, some children will scribble; some will draw; some will write a few letters, words, or a sentence; some will write their names. Some will copy your picture. Some will copy your sentences. Regardless of its nature, it is a major accomplishment: the child has produced a written piece and believes he can write.

Some children, however, will not write at all. Kindergartners may start to cry, hide under the tables, suck their thumbs, or cling to you. Cope with these latter children as you walk around and talk to children who are making an attempt to write. Encourage students as you go, bringing the clingers with you as an audience.

Say encouraging things to your writers as they work, such as:
> *I like the way you used a purple crayon.*
> *What are you writing about?*
> *What a pretty tree!*

Can you tell me what this is?
The letter C for your cat is this one... pointing to C on an ABC strip taped to the
table or desk.

Eventually, by seeing their peers' work and from hearing your encouragement, the non-writers will want to write too, and they will come to believe that they can.

What comes next

After five to ten minutes, gather the class at the Author's Chair. (During the next week, you will have a formal How-to-Get-to-Author's-Chair model and practice. See Chapter 4.) Place your chair beside the Author's Chair. Ask writers if they would like to share their writing in the Author's Chair. Share your writing first, as a model. Point to your drawing and read the writing. Ask them what part they liked the best.

Now, listen to four to six children and praise their efforts. *I like the way you told about your dog; Using crayons is fun, isn't it?; That was interesting about your tooth; I like the way you made that circle; I like the way you made that M.* Thank the volunteers for sharing their writing. This is your first model for giving compliments. Complimenting good writing is an important aspect of a supportive writing community. You will find a complete description of modeling Author's Chair and compliments in Chapter 7.

Remember that all forms of writing are acceptable: random marks, drawings, vertical or horizontal scribbling, strings of letters, letter or word labels, strings of words.

Additional sharing

Invite all students to read their writing to one other classmate before they put it away. Show them where they will keep their writing. Give them time to share and to put their papers away. Let the children put their own papers in the storage area or ask a student to collect the papers. Though this takes a few more minutes than if you did it, it will develop a sense of ownership and responsibility. It will also give children a chance to get up and stretch. (Eventually, to streamline writing-workshop closure, have children put their work away one group at a time.) Remind students that they will write again tomorrow.

You have now launched your daily writing workshop and established a number of important concepts.

- You have indicated to your students that they will write every day.
- You have modeled writing.
- They have seen that they must choose their own topic.
- They have seen that they will have a chance to share.
- They have seen you accept their early efforts.

Watch them turn into writers.

The Second Day

On the following day, write children's names on the back of their papers before distributing them. Or, instead of distributing separate papers, staple 6-10 papers together with a colorful paper cover for a first journal. The stapled-paper journals will form a record of children's progress if pages are dated.

Later in the year, children can use real notebooks for their daily writing. The downside of giving young children a composition or spiral-bound notebook in the first week of school is they will often color and mark randomly on every page and use the book up lickety-split. I like to start with recycled, unlined paper until the students learn the procedures of daily writing workshop. From the first day of school, I provide free access to the recycled paper — the more children handle writing tools and make marks, the quicker they will be ready for writing.

Starting the Second Day of Writing Workshop

Gather the class at the easel and ask children if they know what they will write about today. Encourage those who do to tell the class. Thank them. Invite the ones who know what they will write to pair up for today's writing. Send them to their desks or tables. Keep the remaining children with you to start the writing time.

Writing time

Sit at a table or in a circle at the easel with the remaining children. If your floor is carpeted, pass out clipboards with paper already attached. (Some paired writers will want clipboards, too; show all the writers where they are stored.)

Put your paper on the easel or table and begin to draw and label the elements with starting consonants, talking as you write. Choose a mundane topic. Children need to know they can write about anything.

This is about my house. Label it **H**. *It has a tree in front.* Label it **T**. *I had to paint my house this summer. Can you guess what color I painted it? That's me painting my house.* Write beneath your picture: This is me painting my house. I am painting it blue.

Your Model: Draw your picture here and write out your monologue for the modeled writing for Day Two. Tab this page to find it quickly.

Invite the children to do their own drawing and writing. Send them off with partners to talk and write.

Some children will not join a partner or begin writing. Stay with them and ask each one to tell you something. Take dictation in the form of a simple drawing and labeling. Label the main element of the drawing with a whole word. It is a word they have articulated and is important to them. Give them back their papers to hold and read to each other. Invite them to trace over their key word (using any writing tool) or color the picture while you help other writers.

If time remains, work your way around to the children who paired up, and talk to them briefly. Bring non-writers with you, holding their hands to form a chain.

What do you say? Try something like this:
Do you like to write with markers? I like pencils best.
Oh, I have a cat, too!

I like your drawing.
How is your writing coming along?
My mom has black hair, too.
How did you think of your idea?
Is that your house?
Here is how you make a J, just like in your name. Point to child's name.

When I first started teaching writing, I used to carry these questions and comments around with me on a cue card. I was nervous about what to say to young writers. In no time at all, I learned which ones worked best — the ones that writers responded to with conversation about their writing. With practice, you will find which ones work best for you and your writers.

There may be children who will not talk or answer. Do not make an issue of it. Give them an encouraging smile and move on.

Closing the writing workshop

When you see that the majority of students are ready, repeat the first-day's sharing procedure (Author's Chair) and the closing routine in which children share their writing with one another before they put their papers away. You do not need to conduct Author's Chair in every session once you have established the daily writing workshop. I recommend using it each day for the first week, however, to encourage youngsters to write and share.

Analyze children's writing

Analyze your children's work from the first two days to find out what level writer they are and what mechanical skills they have. That is, does a child make a mark of any kind, draw lines or closed figures, draw recognizable objects or people, scribble, make some letters, write his or her name, write words, or write sentences? (See Emergent and Early Developing Writing Stages, page xii.)

From this diagnosis, you will be able to judge which students are emergent writers and which ones are developing writers. This diagnosis will help you plan writing lessons and models. Most kindergartens and first grades include both emergent and developing writers.

The Rest of the Year

At this point, you may be saying: *This seems chaotic.* Or asking: *What is happening? What about the children who aren't able to do anything? What about the ones who are asking me,* "How do you spell...?" "How do you make a letter?"

I have asked you to jump into a daily, whole-class writing workshop in order to establish the expectations, attitudes, and behavior that underlie every successful writing community. After the first three days, your community will not be functioning smoothly, but you will have shown children that you believe they can write.

In subsequent daily writing workshops you will model the procedures they will need to operate in a community of writers. You will show them how printed text works; how to draw pictures and tell about them; how to match their language sounds to the symbols that represent them. You will help them solve the puzzle of writing and written text.

If we wait to start writing instruction until after most of the children have learned to form all their letters and know all their sound-to-symbol connections, we will have missed the chance to let need drive the acquisition of writing skills. Daily writing workshop creates that need.

Chapter 3
Conducting the Daily Writing Workshop

The daily writing workshop should last about 45 minutes. We have seen that it is made up of three components: a starting activity, the writing time, and the sharing time. The time devoted to each component will vary. For instance, on one day you might devote a significant block of time to a starting lesson and close with a brief sharing time.

On another day, the starting activity might consist only of reminding students about using a writing skill that was introduced in a previous lesson. Sharing time might then be longer with five or six young writers presenting their work in Author's Chair.

During the first few weeks, spend time modeling and practicing writing workshop procedures. You may need two months or more to train your children in these procedures. No matter how long it takes, this training is necessary if your daily writing workshop is to run smoothly. The relevant models are described in the next chapter, What Children Need to Know about Writing Workshop.

The following chart should help you envision a daily writing workshop.

Daily Writing Workshop

Starting Component: 2-20 minutes

Starting Activities might include a lesson, modeled writing, reading aloud for a literature model, choral reading, or a class discussion with shared writing. (You will find lessons and other starting activities throughout the book.) If the starting activity is brief, the sharing component can be extended, and vice versa.

Writing Component: 15-20 minutes

During the writing session, children are actively writing, with or without your guidance.

Students are:	Teacher is:
Drawing and talking: prewriting.	Roving to encourage, guide, and help.
Writing	Conferencing with individual writers.
Dictating a piece to you.	Taking dictation.
Working in a group with the teacher.	Conducting a group lesson that includes writing, with four to five writers

Sharing Component: 5-12 minutes

Author's Chair for three to four children — not every session, not every writer.

Each writer sharing with one other writer before putting writing away — every session.

The Starting Component

The starting component of your daily writing workshop takes one of many forms: the class choral reading of a Big Book, practicing workshop procedures, discussing writing and the writing process, shared writing of a class piece, your reading to children, reminding children about a target skill from a previous lesson, modeling writing at the easel, or introducing a new skill in a lesson.

Most teachers present an extended whole-class lesson once a week and use short starting components (mainly modeled writing) during the rest of the week. This ensures that children will have ample writing time each session.

Starting with a Lesson

Here is an example of a lesson (10 minutes long) to start the writing component. It is from *Tere Matrisciano, master kindergarten teacher, Lincoln Elementary School, Caldwell, New Jersey.*

When some of your children are writing strings of scribbles or letters, and those strands have a scribble- or letter-to-word-correspondence, they are ready for a lesson in **finger spacing**.

- Gather your writers at the easel and tell them you were reading their work and had trouble understanding some of them. Show them a sample paper with writing consisting of an unbroken strand of consonants. IHADGAHZF (This reads: *I have a dog and he is funny*). Have a prepared copy of it on easel paper ready for this lesson.

- Read it as fast as you can with the words slurred together: *Ihaveadogandheisfunny*. (Exaggerate, of course). Repeat it. Look surprised and puzzled. Point out how hard it is to understand the writing when you read it in that fashion.

- Now show your children a page from a Big Book that they know well. Read a sentence slowly. Have them read it with you. Point out the spaces between each word. Or, have a student point to the spaces with a pointer. Call them finger spaces. Say, *This is what writers do to help their readers separate the words.*

- Next, rewrite the IHADGAHZF piece on the easel paper, letter by letter, with finger spaces between each letter. As you write it, have the children re-read it with you. Suggest how it would sound with finger spaces. *I, H (have), A, DG(dog), A (and), H (he), Z (is), F (funny). I H A DG A H Z F*

- Show the children a set of tongue depressors you have previously decorated with fingernails at the ends.

- Go over the *I H A DG A H Z F* piece, placing a tongue-depressor finger-spacer between the letters as you re-read it. Have the children read along with you.

- Suggest they might like to use these decorated finger sticks or their own finger to put spaces between their *words*. Give sticks to the children who want to use them.

- Start the writing session.

- Afterwards, in Author's Chair, have fellow writers give a thumbs-up, silent signal to any writers who used finger spacing between their marks, letters, or words.

Now this idea is out in your writing community. Some children will incorporate it into their writing work; others will not. The children who use finger spaces will often point out to their writing partners when they need finger spaces. Authors will be under peer pressure to use finger spaces if they want to be read and understood.

Starting with Modeled Writing

In **modeled writing**, you compose in front of the class to demonstrate print-text conventions and writing skills. You can use the blackboard, an easel, or an overhead projector. You will think aloud, talking to the children about the things you consider as you compose. For example, to model wrapping text, you might write two sentences about a picture or your drawing. You might say, *Whoops, I'm at the end of the line and I didn't finish what I was telling. Where shall I continue my writing?*

Modeling Text Wrapping

Text wrapping is a crucial concept to model. In many classrooms Daily Messages and Daily Oral Language (DOL) sentences are always written in a list of single sentences. Children may never see the teacher use the wrapping principle. As a result, many of them develop Single Sentence Syndrome, a "disease" characterized by meager, undeveloped writing. If we want children to elaborate and write several cohesive sentences on a topic, we must model it often.

In first grade and thereafter, DOL should be presented in paragraph form, even if it consists of just two related sentences.

Draw, write, and memorize your models before it's time to use them. Use the spaces provided throughout this book to create them. Tab their pages to find them quickly. Eventually, you will want to create a collection of models for all your demonstrations and lessons, keeping them in a notebook, arranged by genre or skill. As an additional source, use transparencies of student work that demonstrates the use of a skill. Ask your colleagues to collect good samples and to share them with you. Keep these in your notebook.

Starting with a Literature Model

Start writing workshop by reading from a book or magazine article that demonstrates how an author uses a skill you are teaching your class. You can, for example, read:

- Big Books to demonstrate printed text concepts
- *Ranger Rick* magazines to demonstrate how authors of science articles often use a question for the first sentence, a hook to get their readers interested
- non-fiction books to show children how authors clump related pictures and facts together on a page or on consecutive pages
- personal, narrative-style fiction books (written in the first person and a child's voice to tell the story) to show children how authors describe what happened (see page 113)

Starting with Shared Writing

An effective way to start daily writing workshop after the whole class has had a common experience, is with **shared writing**. This means you compose a piece in front of the class while children contribute words and sentences. A field trip, physical education activity, an assembly, a visitor (person or pet), a new book, an art project, a program on TV, or a theme study, such as animals, oceans, food, etc., are all experiences that lend themselves to a class piece.

Talking about a common experience and listing key words is a perfect prewriting activity. Before the shared writing, help students arrange the list in either time sequence for a narrative piece or by list/linking (grouping the words that go together) for an informational expository piece.

With children contributing sentences about the key words, write the piece in front of the students on easel paper or newsprint. The list and the piece should be displayed afterward for children to review the vocabulary and to identify their contributions.

Here are some questions and comments to get things going.

What do you think..., Should we include..., How about..., Where shall we put..., What about..., Remember ..., I like the way you put two things together that were about the same thing.

> We went to a farm. We saw a cow.
> We saw pigs. A pig licked Jessica's
> knee. We rode in a wagon. A tractor
> pulled it.

As you construct the piece, skip lines so you can insert things children remember later in the discussion that are related to something already written. Be sure to demonstrate the wrapping of text, as shown above.

Use **shared writing** to reinforce print principles: the left-to-right movement of text, the wrapping principle, or the convention of ending a statement with a period. Talk aloud as you write to show what things you think about as you write. For instance: *I need to leave a finger space here; I need to put a period here because I just finished what you said; I want to write more, so I will start again on the next line.* When you model these principles, the children who are ready to use them will start to incorporate them in their own writing.

Be sure to display the finished class piece at the children's eye level. Invite them to find the word(s) they contributed. Put their initials next to those words.

Underline **content words**, the words particular to the topic. Most teachers make a chart of these words to accompany the class piece or highlight them with markers. Content words are the first words children will be responsible for spelling correctly when you introduce editing for spelling in the second half of first grade. Content words are found in the classroom environmental text (words, lists of words, charts, i.e., the highlighted writing on the classroom walls and furniture) or the books children use when they write about things they know or are studying.

The content words in the shared-writing example above are underlined here:

> *We went to a <u>farm</u>. We saw a <u>cow</u>.*
> *We saw <u>pigs</u>. A pig licked Jessica's*
> *knee. We rode in a <u>wagon</u>. A <u>tractor</u>*
> *pulled it.*

Starting with an Activity

Instead of reading, modeling, or presenting a lesson, you might move naturally into your writing session from a project the children are doing. For example, after reading about skunks, children might make paper-bag skunk puppets, and then write about a skunk doing something. Go directly to the writing component and do not interrupt their momentum and engagement with the project. You can extend the activity further by having them act out with their puppets what they wrote.

Transition to the writing component

If the starting component is longer than 15 minutes, you should provide children with an opportunity to move about for a minute or two before they begin the writing component. They might stretch, sing a ditty about writing, stand and tell you what they are planning to write, gather their materials, and arrange their supplies, tables or desks, etc.

The Writing Component

The writing component of daily workshop should last 15-20 minutes. It must always include **guided** or **independent writing**, along with prewriting (talking, drawing, making lists), or conferencing with you.

CAUTIONARY NOTE:

Copying text from the blackboard or a book does not count as guided or independent writing.

In **guided writing**, the children write and you respond — helping, encouraging, teaching. You do this as you walk around, stopping to talk briefly to writers, trying to get to as many writers as you can. You can also do this in group conferences with writers who are working on a common skill or in scheduled, individual conferences for specific help.

Independent writing is just what it says: writers working without your guidance. They may, however, use peers for help. See details about getting help in Chapter 4.

Writing partnerships

Young writers talk as they draw and write, and they need to share what they compose. They help each other with letter formation, drawing, or writing a word.

Partners work beside or across from each other; they do no work on the same paper. They often write about the same thing, and some will copy from each other. That is acceptable to start. Later, you will help these children find their own topics.

You might assign partnerships arbitrarily to start. When you are familiar with children's writing abilities and behavior, pair students who work well together. Non-writers often need a writer as a partner. ESOL students need an articulate, talkative English-speaking partner. Some young writers find another who is just right and ask to be partners. If some children can't work together, assign them other partners.

The Sharing Component

The sharing component of daily writing workshop is a chance for all writers to hear their writing. This is an important part of the writing process and your writing program. When young writers read what they wrote (early emergent writers may "tell" about their drawings), they get a sense of authorship. They develop confidence in what they know. They are heard. They count.

During the first weeks of writing workshop, you will use the sharing component to model Author's Chair and peer conferences. Adjust workshop components to allow for the time this will take.

Author's Chair is a whole-class activity. Three to six young writers read their pieces, sitting in the special Author's chair. With your guidance at first, their classmates compliment them and ask questions. You can use Author's Chair to model responses that are helpful to the writer and point out how a writer has used a skill. For an extensive description of how to conduct Author's Chair, see Chapter 7.

Close every writing session with children sharing their work with one other child. The children who did not present in Author's Chair need the chance to hear their work. Designate a place such as a carpeted area or a space in front of the class easel, for children to gather and share writing. Remind them as they put their writing away that they will be writing again the next day.

Chapter 4
What Children Need to Know About Writing Workshop

Invest time and effort in establishing daily writing-workshop procedures. It will pay off by creating the environment you need to teach students to write. Young children need to know what is expected of them and how to operate in their classroom writing community. They have to know how to function in a group, taking responsibility for personal behavior that enhances, rather than distracts from, the learning environment.

Basic rules of conduct in the primary daily writing workshop include:
- getting materials and supplies quietly
- keeping voices under control during peer conferences and prewriting activities
- finding help when the teacher is busy
- knowing what to do when finished with a task

Here are several important procedures you will want to practice with your youngsters in the first months of school.

How to Hold a Pencil

You need to show kindergarten children how to hold a pencil. If children learn it on their own, they often will hold pencils in strange ways. Reinforce the most common, comfortable position. Send your left-handed students to a left-handed teacher for instruction. They will appreciate learning from a fellow southpaw.

How to Write Manuscript (Printed) Letters

One of the best ways to model forming alphabet letters is with a gross-muscle activity. By that I mean forming the letters using the whole arm, not just pencil-gripping fingers. Model the direction of the movement involved in forming letters, including the starting point.
- Trace letters in the air.
- Give your students one-inch brushes and paint letters in water on the concrete outside. You will be in charge of a bucket of water. (Remember to tell your custodial staff about this activity before you do it.)
- Invite children to use the blackboard to write large letters with chalk. Print large models in another color chalk for them to trace.
- Use wooden pattern blocks that provide a knob and a track for children to trace letter shapes in the correct sequence of the curved and straight components. See Bibliography for source.

How to Move to the Class Easel or Author's Chair

Seating arrangements

Show children the aids you are utilizing to mark the seating arrangement. Carpet pieces define space and ease sitting on cold, hard floors. On carpeted floors, delineate seating rows with masking tape or each seat with an X of duct tape to help children sit and space themselves quickly and with a minimum of fuss.

Practice moving quietly

Ask the children to return to their desks or tables and tell them you are going to have them practice going to the Class Easel or Author's Chair quickly and quietly. You might call them by table-group name or number, desk area, colors of clothing, or by name. Whatever method you subsequently use, vary the order each day so that all children get a chance to sit in the first row.

Go through the drill twice. They will like the movement. Praise their success in getting to the spot quickly and quietly.

How to Get Help When the Teacher is Busy

Practice the procedures a writer should follow to get your help with the least disruption to the rest of the writing community. I don't need to tell you how important this is. Egocentric kindergartners and first graders demand our constant attention. They need our attention often. But our job is to encourage independence. We must show children how to cope when we cannot attend to them.

To keep interruptions to a minimum during conferencing, all young writers must have acceptable means of getting help while you are busy. Students need to know when you *are not* available and they need to know when you *are* available.

Kindergarten teacher, Tere Matrisciano, wears a "Magic Scarf" around her neck when she is conferencing with young writers. The others recognize this as a signal not to interrupt. If children need her help, they sit at the class meeting area and wait for her. While they are there, they can share their writing with others waiting.

As Tere moves around the room, she checks between conferences to see if there is a student waiting there. She helps that child before moving on to the next conference. Her children have been trained not to interrupt a conference, how to get help from other students, and what to do while they wait for her.

Where to find things

Supplies must be accessible. Writing-workshop supplies include: books, writing tools, paper and surfaces, letters, and words.

Help from the community

Children need to know that they can ask other children for help. During writing time they should be free to go to another child, a word bank, the class library, or environmental print to get the help they need. This means there will be movement during writing workshop. You will need to set parameters for this movement: direct routes, time limits, lowered voices, etc.

As you learn more about your young writers, arrange student partnerships to foster peer teaching. Matching peers by common interests and knowledge, spellers with non-spellers or two writers working on the same genre or topic, increases the opportunity for young writers to help and support one another.

From memory, try to make a list of all your students and the things you know about them. If you can come up with the entire class and significant things about them — their interests, what they know — you are ready to guide the class toward symbiotic peer partnerships.

How to Get Help with Writing a Letter, a Word, or Drawing a Picture

Notice that I say, help *writing* a word, not, help *spelling* a word. This is deliberate. I encourage all young writers to ask, *How do I write the word...?* This encourages children to use their phonics knowledge, their sound-to-symbol strategies, and to approximate the spelling of a needed word so they can get on with their writing.

An undue emphasis on spelling while a child is *learning to write* is counterproductive to writing development. As a result of their concern for spelling words correctly, children limit their writing to words they can spell, not to words they can say. We want them to be able to use all the words they know, not just those they can spell.

A common strategy children use when they need help *writing* a word is to ask the teacher or another child. Here are some classroom procedures that encourage children to help each other.

The help strip

During writing workshop, young writers may need help drawing as well as writing. The following model describes a concrete approach, the Help Strip, to provide that help and foster peer teaching.

Materials you will need:
- Large strips of paper (doctor's examination-table paper, opened paper bags, brown paper)
- Crayons or markers
- A place to spread the strip during writing time

During the second week of school, as a starting component to a writing workshop, model your picture-writing. Talk about the elements in your drawing. *I went to a farm. I saw a pig. Oh, no! I don't know how to draw a pig. Can one of you draw a pig? Jared, you can? Will you show me how?*

Show the children the strip of paper you taped to the wall, a desk, or the floor. Call it the **Help Strip**. Gather the students around and ask Jared to draw a pig on the strip. Thank Jared. Now, trace over Jared's pig drawing. Then draw the pig again on your own, also on the help strip. Now go back to the easel and complete your picture-writing with a pig picture. Label it **P**.

Demonstrate the Help Strip again the next day, this time using it for getting help writing a letter or word. As you model writing say, *I want to write the word fish? Who can show me how to write it?* Have a child take you to the strip and write the word *fish*. (If the child writes just an F or some temporary spelling, accept it.) Thank the writer. Trace over the letter or word. Take your paper over to the help strip and use the word as a model to write *fish* on your paper.

In a few weeks, have two students demonstrate this model again. Ask a child who can draw a house (or anything) to do it on the Help Strip. Ask a child who wants to learn how to draw a house to watch and to trace or practice on the strip. Remind them to thank each other.

Encourage students to use the Help Strip both for drawing and writing help. Devise a signal system for when the Help Strip is operative (times when you are not to be interrupted). Praise the children who use this coping strategy.

Designated helpers

Place movable signs such as **Designated Letter Helper, Word Helper, Drawing Helper,** on two or three children's chairs during each writing session. Start with children who have some command of the sound-to-symbol relationship, can make some of their letters, can write or find words around the room, or who can draw. Tell students that everyone will have a chance to be a designated helper.

Change the signs daily or weekly. Make badges or some signal mechanism for designated helpers to wear. (Hats are not a good idea, hygienically speaking.)

Emergent writers helping each other will not necessarily come up with the correct drawing, letters, or spelling for a word. But encourage designated helpers to show classmates where to look on the walls, in word banks, in books, on charts. They will often be wrong, especially early on, but that's all right. The important training is that children learn to use other resources besides you.

When children know they will have a turn at being a designated helper, they take it seriously and try to help. Reading the environmental print on your classroom walls, practicing writing their letters, and putting words on class charts all contribute to child's ability to perform as a designated helper. Encourage children to read the walls with a periodic field trip around the room. Children like to learn on the move.

What to Do When You Finish Your Writing

Young writers finish at different times within a writing period. While they await Author's Chair, or any other ending ritual of your daily writing workshop, they need to know what to do. While writing workshop is in session, all their options should relate to language arts, rather than free play. Additionally, when students finish other work during the day, they should have the opportunity to return to their writing. Writing folders should be readily accessible.

Here are some options you might give writers:

- Read your piece to another student who is finished. Do that in the designated sharing spot. (Rug area in front of the easel, corner table, special seats, etc.)
- Hold a three- or four-writer Author's Chair on your own. (Model this for students after they have had experience with whole-class Author's Chair.)
- Look at picture books.
- Cut pictures and words from magazines and newspapers. Paste them on a sheet of paper and tell someone about them.
- Listen to a book on tape in the listening center.
- Circle letters or words you recognize in a big-print book or in a writing-in-this-is-allowed book. This needs to be modeled (see the chart on the next page) before you make it an option.

Noise Level

Have no doubt about it: your students will generate noise during writing workshop. But it must not be so noisy that writers can't work. Establishing and practicing the procedures that make the workshop run smoothly will control the noise level. Dividing the room into Quiet! Writers at Work, and Conference zones also helps. In a well constructed classroom-writing workshop, students are engaged with their writing, and excessive noise is not usually an issue.

Letter and Word-recognition Model

Materials: pages from large-print magazine or books, highlighting marker, date stamp and ink pad

- Make a chart-size block of text, or enlarge a page from a big-print Reader's Digest. Put it on an overhead transparency.

- Show your class how to find a word they know by sight. Start with the word *and*. Run your finger along the lines of print on the overhead projection or at the easel. Have the children tell you to stop when they see an *and*. Circle the word. If they select an *and* that is part of another word such as stand, hand, land, that's okay, too.

- Next, have the children count the circled *ands*. Put that number on the top of the page and date stamp it.

- Invite the children to try this on their own. Give them a single page of big-print magazine text.

- They may work in writing-buddy pairs or alone.

- Children might color in the circles of the letters *a, b, d, g, o, p, q*, or, circle letters that occur in their own names.

You might give each child a big-print page each week. Have them circle the words they recognize and count the circled words each time. Keep the collection, and note the increasing number of words they recognize for your own records.

This is not an assessment activity. This is an inventorying activity. Children like inventorying, listing what they know. You see evidence of it in their early writing. *I lv mm, I lov mi dad, I lov miss Landrum, I luv dgs, I lov red.* Praise the children when they circle new words. Display children's completed pages.

Sharing Technique: Peers Complimenting Fellow Writers

Whenever you call on children during writing practice to share what they have accomplished, use this community-building technique. Instead of calling on writers to tell what wonderful thing they did, call on their peer partners. *Who heard your partner use a color word, a number word, the target skill? Please tell us your partner's name and what he wrote.*

In this sharing technique, young writers broadcast examples of their partner's good writing. This contributes to the pool of writing knowledge. The technique fosters critical listening and reinforces awareness of the target skill. When peers give the compliments for achievement, it builds respect and a sense of community.

In schools dedicated to writing education, training children in writing-workshop procedures begins in kindergarten and continues through every grade. Teachers in these schools report that students come into their classes at the start of the year ready to write. They speak the language of a writing community. They know the language of the writing process. They expect to write — *When will we have Author's Chair? Where would you like me to put this rough draft? I'm using temporary spelling for this word. What is the target skill for this writing? I need a peer conference.*

Section Two: The Writing Process In the Primary Grades

Chapter 5
Prewriting

Prewriting is about choosing a topic and gathering your thoughts, followed by rehearsing and planning how to present those thoughts. Young writers use talking and drawing as their main prewriting activity. Their talking and drawing leads them to their topics and provides the visual stimuli for details about it.

Topic Choice: Personal-based Writing

Educational publishing abounds with cute, motivational story starters. This is due to a misconception that children wont write because they can't think of a topic, and that if we can just give them a great topic, they will write. This is a false premise. Young children have plenty of ideas; just listen to them talk. The main reason many children won't write is they don't know how.

All good writing instruction starts with personal writing as the vehicle. Primary-grade youngsters are strongly egocentric and eager to write about themselves and what they know. When they are encouraged and provided with the skills to do so, they write uninhibitedly and with great variety.

We must show young writers that we believe they have something to say. We must help them tap into their personal experiences, expertise, and interests. If we select topics for them and provide story starters, we send young writers a message: You are not able to pick meaningful topics. It doesn't take very many *Let's all write a Leprechaun story for St. Patrick's Day or Everybody write a Magic Snowflake story*, to lose young writers. I have seen it happen all too frequently.

Elaboration, a main goal of primary writing education, is directly proportional to how much a writer knows about his subject.

When children write about themselves, they know all the facts and events. In short, they have control over the material. This means they can concentrate on the acts of composing and writing. It means they will write in greater detail than they would on a topic they know little about. They have the potential for elaborate writing, rich with details. In addition, it means they are engaged, raising the probability they will stay on task.

With an effective program of primary writing instruction, most children can become fluent writers. When they enter the intermediate grades, they will be ready to master the important skill of writing in response to an assigned topic or prompt. The purpose of that exercise is as much to evaluate the students' knowledge or understanding of the topic as it is to evaluate their writing. (Young writers should be encouraged to regard it as a chance to show off their growing skills.)

Lessons and Models

What I Know

Help young writers build lists or inventories of what they know best.

Model it first

Take the time to create a list of your own interests, experiences, places you have been, things you collect, what you know. You need models at your fingertips. Memorize your model. When you use it to show students your strategy for choosing a topic, you will re-create it as if you are making it up as you go, thinking aloud. You will probably add to your list as you model — it happens naturally. Remember topics that get the children thinking and add them to your memorized model.

Be sure to list ordinary things. Children who have been fed story-starters or have had topics given to them, may think their ideas are not exciting enough to write about. Encourage writers to focus on their personal expertise.

Sample model monologue

Let me see. What shall I write about? ... My dog did the funniest thing this morning. I could write about that. (Write Dog on your list.) *Let me see. What do I know a lot about? Horses..., knitting..., Vermont..., the beach! I was just there last weekend and saw a dolphin.* (Write beach on your list.) *I collect teddy bears. And I've been fishing..., I've been to a museum..., and to a county fair. That was where I first saw llamas. The kids in 4-H were showing them. Have you ever been to a fair?*

Illustrate your list with little pictures as a model for the early-stage emergent writers who draw instead of write.

Your model

Write your list model below. Tab this page of the book to find it easily when you model your first list.

List	Write your monologue here

Now the children join in

Gather your class at the easel. Ask children to list what they know, in oral form. The object of the activity is for them to talk about what they know, for classmates to learn about each other, and for you to show them you value what they know.

Give young writers time to make their own lists, as you did for your model, in picture and written form. For all listing activities, supply students with long strips of sturdy paper, 4-5 inches wide — **a list should look like a list**. A good source of list paper is a printing shop. Call and ask the manager to save some card-stock scraps for you. Show children how to draw the activity, place, or object if they cannot write some letters. (See also **Picture Lists** below.)

When your young writers have a few entries, ask volunteers to share their lists. Ask the students to star one or two listed items that they might like to write about later. Give out star stickers or colored labels for them to indicate their choices (a concrete aid). The act of listing causes young writers to *think* about the things they know that interest them.

All ideas are acceptable. The object is not to see who can make the longest list. A list of three to four entries is fine. Encourage writers to add to their list at anytime.

Some teachers assign making this **What I Know** list for homework, which brings parents into the process.

Picture Lists: Children love to make picture lists. Start another writing workshop session with picture list making. Gather magazines and have students cut out pictures of activities they can do, things they collect, places they have been, or experiences they have had. Ask them to paste the pictures on large sheets of paper, opened paper bags, or the back of wrapping paper or wallpaper. Young writers will need to store this collection in their writing box, file, folder, or bag. They should add to it whenever they can.

You can also take their lists through dictation and add little drawings to help them remember the items. In addition, you can ask parents to help their children make this picture list — writing the words, drawing for them, or helping them find pictures.

Activities in a picture list might include:
- shopping
- eating at a fast-food place
- flying a kite
- dancing
- singing
- making toast
- biking
- skating
- drawing
- fishing
- crossing a street
- having a bandage put on a finger

Children can use this picture list during lessons and for writing activities, as well as for choosing a topic. Some applicable activities are:

- adding written labels, words, or sentences to the pictures
- responding to a lesson about verbs and *ing: The kids are eating cereal.*
- choosing attributes about the content of the pictures for descriptive target skills: *The kid has a blue shirt.*
- publishing an I-CAN-DO class book

List Anything

Invite writers to make a list of *anything*. Emergent writers naturally pass through an inventorying stage as they learn to write, making lists of symbols and letters they know, families of words, words they can spell.

I love my M. (I love my Mom.)
I love my cat
I love my dog
I love my bruver.

All learners retain that urge to inventory and should have the opportunity to satisfy it by making lists.

First-grade teacher, Lisa Jaswoskowski, Manatee County, FL, puts her students through a choral exercise as they prepare to write in science. Accompanying themselves with pantomiming arm movements, they chant: "First, we gather the information. Next, we sort the information. Then, we write the information."

Lisa started a list-making session in her class by reading from the book, I Love Lists, by Linda Schwartz, (The Learning Works, CA, 1988.) Lisa modeled a list of her own. Then, she talked to her students about their chant, and how list makers sort and put things together that go together. Finally, she invited children to tell what they wanted to list.

One girl selected endangered species, other boys and girls selected states (using maps), grown animals and babies, colors, ice cream flavors. They used long strips of paper for their lists. Soon they were all busy, helping one another, using environmental text, and sharing their lists.

Make a bulletin board full of lists. Show children how to make a title for their lists.

Catherine ☆
Catherine Faivrit things
Too Wash
& arch Magic8Cooll Bus
STRT Wrss
The Pwor Dome

Catherines
Faivrit things
To Doo
Skate Datch
Sing Smiad

Tace Pixrs
Ice Cream

The Value of Lists

- List making is easy. When the task is simply to write single words, young writers who have difficulty writing sentences can excel.

- List making is classification — sorting things into groups based on common traits. This is a critical-thinking skill and should be used in the writing workshop to support science, social studies, and math.

- List making leads to vocabulary expansion. Children get words from other children, you, the environment, and books.

- List making can lead to publishing. Try a class BOOK OF LISTS, with each child contributing a list. Younger writers might make a list and publish their own books, with an illustration and one word to a page.

   Your class can find such listables as

   colors, clothes, girls' names, games, boys' names, numbers, birds, food, fruit, fish, vegetables, machines, tools, sports, animals, jobs, streets, dinosaurs, ice cream flavors, endangered species, toys, teams, teachers, thing they like about a friend.

What is Everyone Else Doing?

During the first weeks of writing workshop, ask those who chose topics to share them with the class and tell how they decided to write about those topics. Writers, new to choosing topics, need to hear what topics other children choose.

Personal Interview

Interview children to help them find their areas of personal expertise. Write their lists on cards and help the students read them. Before they leave you, have them select one of the topics for the day's writing.

Clipboard Trip

If first graders are having trouble finding a topic, send them around the room during writing workshop with a class list on a clipboard to find out *what topics* others have chosen. Use their survey results for your own records. Their interaction with each writer counts as a peer conference for that child.

Topics from Pictures and Books

Children find topics related to their personal knowledge in art prints, magazine photographs, personal snapshots, and literature. Read both non-fiction and fiction books to children. When you read a narrative, lead the children to discuss the characters, the problem, or the theme. Help them compare the character to themselves. Help them compare things they have done to what the character did. Help them compare what they know about a subject with what they heard in the book.

When they can say things like this — *I have a grandmother like that; My Mom works, too; I went to a fair, too; I lost my teddy bear once; I went to the hospital just like that kid; I think there's something under my bed just like the boy in that book. I have a hat just like that* — they can write about them.

Repetitive Topics

Young writers often will use a topic repetitively, which is fine. It gives them a comfortable and secure vehicle on which to apply new writing skills. (Just think what might have happened to Steven Farley if his publisher had complained about receiving yet another black stallion story.)

Even though we encourage and show them how to chose their own topics, some children will, from time to time, get stuck trying to choose one. They may fall into the trap of copying other children's choices with the inevitable frustration and loss of engagement that happens when writers have limited knowledge about their topic. Let this happen. Then, be sure to point out to them why they became bored or gave up on the writing. This is a good lesson itself.

Gathering Thoughts and Rehearsing

Children jump right into their writing as soon as they get an idea. They draw or write it and say, *I'm done*. If we want young writers to elaborate — to write several sentences about a topic — we must encourage them to talk before they write.

If You Can Talk, You Can Write

When young writers talk as they draw or study a picture, they are gathering their thoughts and rehearsing what they will write. (Actually, all writers, novice and expert, talk to rehearse what they will write.) Graham Wallas, in *The Art of Thought*, said, "The little girl had the makings of a poet in her who, being told to be sure of her meaning before she spoke, said, '*How can I know what I think until I see what I say?*'"

The more young writers talk about their topic, the more they write. **Elaboration is directly proportional to the amount of prewriting**. Provide time and opportunity for this important prewriting strategy — talking. No, it will not be as quiet as a library in your room, but you must give up that goal if you want students to make progress in their writing.

Talk Time

Young writers talk time may be informal conversations between partners as they sit and work or it may be a formal ritual with students placing their chairs to sit knee-to-knee, in a conference. Knee-to-knee conferences encourage children to listen to each other and to stay on task. Remind them of the target skill(s) currently under study when they talk to prewrite.

A first-grade class studied ocean life for a month. The teacher showed films, took the class on a field trip to a marine facility, and provided opportunities for reading, listening, and hands-on activities about ocean life.

On a day I visited the class, she gathered the children and asked them to recall all the animals in the sea they had studied or seen. She asked them to select their favorite sea animal, sit knee-to-knee with a partner, and tell each other what they liked about their chosen marine animal, and interesting things about it. She modeled such an exchange with one child, and then sent the children about their task.

As the pairs finished their talking conferences, I could see that they knew what to do next. They went to a supply table for drawing paper, then found a spot for writing with their partners. Most began drawing their favorite animal and continued talking about it. Some started writing immediately.

The teacher circulated through the room and encouraged pairs, referring writers to each other or to wall charts for the spelling of content words (sea mammals and ocean words). Some of the children referred to the Dolch Primary Word List that they kept in their writing folders.

The teacher told me that since she incorporated Talk Time in the writing workshop, the quality and quantity of writing had increased.

Visual Stimuli

Drawing; painting; cutting shapes; pasting and folding paper; looking at magazine pictures, snapshots, and art prints — in other words, using rich visual images — helps children plan what they will write. Their hands, brains, and mouth work together as they compose.

I asked a first grader what she was going to write about today. She answered, "*I don't know; I didn't draw it yet.*"

Graphic Organizers for Emergent Writers

Many graphic planners are abstract in nature, while primary children are in the concrete stage of development. (See your Educational Psychology, Piaget notes from college.) Do not expect emergent and young developing writers to use graphic planners such as clustering or webbing. Webbing is an abstract concept that requires children to use formal thought processes; that usually happens around nine or ten years of age, or older. Do not fall for the many cute ideas that purport to show primary children how to create and use webs or clusters; it is like trying to teach a two-year-old how to tie her shoes. The children are just not ready.

You can, however, introduce them to some activities that help them gather their thoughts and organize them. You can teach them how to create simple information organizers, the simplest of which is a list. You can show them how to record information in charts. And, you can teach them how to physically sort and clump information. (See Chapter 13 for a lesson about physically organizing information.)

Charts

Kathleen Lough, a first-grade teacher in Jefferson Parish, LA, helps her students organize what they know about a topic as they study it in great detail: reading information and fiction books, taking a field trip, talking about pictures, etc. Following a class discussion and using the children's input, Kathleen constructs a chart that organizes the basic facts about the topic. When the class studies animals, children list each animal, and Kathleen records similar information about each one. To help them read the chart and use it, she writes each row in alternating colors. She writes the cat row of information in red, the dog information in blue, the cow information in red, and so forth.

Children choose the animal they will write about, and Kathleen encourages them to add any other information they know.

Animal	What is looks like	What it eats	Where it lives	How it moves
Cat	furry, pointed ears, whiskers, claws that go back in their paws.	birds, mice cat food, fish	in a house	creeps, slinks, walks
Dog	furry, big teeth, claws that are out	bones, meat, dog food	dog house	trots, walks, runs
Cow	big, horns, fur,	grass, hay Etc.	farm	walks

Graphic planners based on sequence, such as storyboards, can be introduced in late first grade when young writers are beginning to understand sequence and beginning to write stories. Model the use of storyboards in analyzing narratives. Some children will start to use them as a literature response tool, but not necessarily to plan their own stories. (See Literature Response in Chapter 13.)

Venn diagrams, a graphic tool for making comparisons, can be modeled in kindergarten and first grade using Hoola Hoops (a concrete aid), but young writers do not use them to organize their expository writing until third and fourth grades (see Chapter 13).

Many primary children are not ready to use graphic organizers to gather their thoughts. To help these children write elaborately, we must encourage them to write about something they know well, provide ample time for prewriting — particularly talking — and model detailed writing for them often.

Chapter 6
Writing

I have called this chapter Writing instead of Drafting because emergent writers do not make successive drafts of a piece. Copying their own work is very difficult for them and becomes onerous. If they want to publish, encourage them to color their drawing more completely, help them tidy their edited manuscript, or arrange for their work to be typed.

Writing Techniques to Model and Encourage

- Model and teach writers to **say what they are writing** as they write it. It is especially difficult for young writers to hold long thoughts while they struggle with the mechanical part of writing.

- Model and encourage young writers to **read what they have written** every few words. This helps them keep their thoughts going. Model this aloud in your own writing. Write, read over, write, read over, change something, read over, write.

- Model and encourage young writers to write **more than a single sentence/thought**.

- **Model writing in a variety of forms** throughout the year: with words consisting of single beginning consonants — *I l m m. S z n.*; with a mixture of words consisting of single beginning consonants plus common sight words from a class word bank — *I like m m. S is n.*; with a words consisting of a beginning consonant and an end consonant plus common sight words — *I like m mm. S is ns.*; with words consisting of all the letters we can hear and sight words *I like mi mm. She is nis.*; with words fully spelled — *I like my mom. She is nice.*

- Encourage Sentence Makers, Information Communicators/Story Makers (stage six and seven emergent writers), and developing writers to **skip lines**. Invite them to use greenbar or bluebar paper for their work. An open manuscript, using this accounting paper, invites revision and allows for it by providing the space.

- Model **drawing a single line through a letter** or word that you decide you did not want to write. Encourage this as early as you can. **Discourage erasing**. *If you erase, you might not be able to think of the word again, and it might be the one you really need.* It is important for writers in the intermediate grades to have developed this habit of looking at writing as something they can change easily, and not looking at these mis-writes as errors.

- Model and encourage using **adhesive labeling material** over messy bits, or tears and holes on the piece. Children can write on these patches.

- Model and encourage **pencils for writing** and colored markers or crayons for drawing.

- Model and encourage **temporary spelling** by training children to ask: *How do you write the word ...?* instead of, *How do you spell the word ...?*

- Show late-stage emergent writers and young developing writers how to **draw a circle or leave a blank** if they can't think of the word they want. This technique parallels a reading strategy we teach children for coping with a new word: read the sentence and skip the word. The syntax of the sentence and what it is about, along with the starting sound, might help you figure out what the new word is.

- Model **imitating the pros**. If your young writers' favorite author starts his work with a question or onomatopoeia, have them try a question or a sound word to start their piece.

- **Staple extra paper** below a drawing when a child's piece grows.

- **Use different paper** for writers in different stages. Small sheets are less intimidating than big ones. Unlined paper is less intimidating than lined paper.

Scottie Ried, a primary teacher at Ben Franklin Science Academy, in Muskogee, Oklahoma, starts first graders journaling on unlined index cards. Then she gives them an unlined half-sheet of paper with one line on it. Then, she gives them the unlined half-sheet with several lines on it. Finally, she gives them fully lined paper.

From Picture Writing to Full Text

To help emergent writers progress from stage to stage, we need to model the writing process, print-text principles, and writing techniques. Young writers need to see the variety of ways they can communicate their ideas, starting with pictures and labels, and moving to full text. Writing is a craft and is learned best by imitation. Teach your children to write through modeling.

Appropriate Models for the Successive Emergent-writing Stages

The following is a list of models that children in each of the seven emergent-writing stages need. You will find descriptions of some of them following the list and the rest throughout the book. Since young writers may exhibit characteristics of several stages at the same time, your models will be previews for some and reviews for others. Your models will be exactly what all young writers need.

The first three stages describe children who have not made the sound-to-symbol connection but are beginning to understand that marks on a paper convey a message.

1. Stage One or Picture Writer

Models:
- choosing a topic
- telling about drawing
- responding orally to pictures for target-skills concept (See Chapter 11)
- labeling elements of a drawing
- using symbols
- making letters — those in a child's name and the starting consonants of his inner words first
- choral reading (use books with repetitive text)
- print principles: left to right movement, finger spaces

2. Stage Two or Verbal Informer

Models:
- responding orally to picture-prompts for target-skill concept
- telling about pictures using targets such as descriptive attributes and telling *what's happening*
- adding details to drawing, telling about them while drawing
- labeling drawings with starting consonants
- writing a two-sentence message below the drawing
- making letters — those in a child's name and starting consonants of his inner words first
- choral reading (use books with repetitive text)
- print principles: left to right movement, finger spaces

3. Stage Three or Letter Copier

Models:
- responding orally to picture-prompts for target-skill concept
- telling about pictures using targets such as descriptive attributes and telling *what's happening*: oral and written
- writing a two-sentence message under drawing, using label letters and symbols
- letter-to-sound connection
- list making
- print principles: left to right, finger spacing, text wrapping
- choral reading (use books with repetitive text)
- stressing the beginning sound of a word
- showing the one-to-one correspondence of written and spoken words using dictation - the child repeats and traces your writing
- list making: symbols and pictures

The following stages describe children who are learning that letters represent language sounds and that words convey meaning.

4. Stage Four or Labeler

Models:
- picture-prompted writing for target-skill concept
- telling about pictures using target skills such as telling what's happening, where things are, and using descriptive attribute of color, number, size
- choral reading (use books with repetitive text)
- print principles: left-to-right, finger spaces, text wrapping
- single starting-consonant writing
- writing two or more related sentences about the topic (drawing)
- list making
- period at the end of all writing

5. Stage Five or Inventory Taker/Sound Maker

Models:
- picture-prompted writing response for target-skill concept
- using target skills
- consonant writing, including blends
- listening for, and adding end sounds
- writing several related sentences
- using finger spaces
- editing by ear for periods at end of sentences

The following stages describe children who understand which letters represent which language sounds, and that words and text follow a standard form.

6. Stage Six or Sentence Maker

Models:
- picture-prompted writing response for target-skill concept
- using target skills in description and informational writing
- list making
- creating titles
- skipping lines
- editing by ear for end punctuation
- writing several related sentences about the topic
- starting a new page for continuing text
- using word banks and environmental text for writing words
- using a question, exclamation, or onomatopoeia for a hook

7. Stage Seven or Information Communicator/Story Maker

Models: all of the stage six models, plus
- additive revision using the ^
- expanding sentences with *where* and *when* phrases
- concrete sorting of information for an expository piece
- using attributes, verbs, comparisons in description
- using transitions in narrative
- capital letter to start sentences and a person's name

Models and Lessons

These following models or lessons can be used any time throughout the day in support of reading and writing. Some are useful as starting components of the daily writing workshop and are marked as such.

Teaching the Letters of the Alphabet

The first letter: The first letter a child needs is the first letter of his or her name. Many children come to school knowing that letter, and often, their whole name. As soon as a child knows that beginning letter, he can write in daily writing workshop. When young writers have their name-starting letter, there may be 10 to 15 different letters known in the writing community. Children can use the Help Strip to show each other those letters. An emergent writer can publish a first book with just one letter: Jessica's first book will have a big J on the cover. Every page will have an J on it and Jessica can illustrate each page. Publishing engenders the feeling of authorship — *Hey, I'm a writer!*

The next letters: Children come to school knowing the sounds of their language. They know and can make the sound of the most of words they use when they talk. (Some can not yet duplicate every sound: th, s, r, and v give some children trouble.) What they have to learn is which letters represent the sounds they know.

The first letters to start matching with sounds are **I**, which the young writer needs immediately to write about himself, and the beginning consonants.

- The first consonants are **b, d, k, m, p, t,** and **s**. These are the ones babies articulate first.
- **N, z, r, l, g, j, h, x, f, v, w, q,** and **y** follow in a general order of increasing difficulty.
- The letters **c** and **g**, with hard and soft versions, are troublesome because they can sound like **s** and **j**. Many children use **k** for the hard **c** through first grade.

- **W, h, q** and **y** are strange because their names certainly don't come close to their sounds. *Double-u* does not sound like **wuh**, *aitch* doesn't sound like **huh**, *cue* doesn't sound like **kwuh**, and *why* doesn't sound like **e, i,** or **yuh**.

Kindergarten student uses the letters of his name to write his message.

Emergent writers, at Stage Four and beyond, begin composing with just a few starting consonants, using a letter-to-word correspondence. Next, they add the end consonants that they hear. Then, they begin to use starting consonant blends and to add median vowels.

Vowels are tricky, with long and short sounds. They are more difficult for children to hear inside a word they are trying to sound out. Introduce the single letter **I** early because emergent writers need that letter as they write about themselves. Teach the other vowels as they are used to *start* common words: **a** is for apple, **e** is for egg, **o** is for open, **u** is for up, **I** is for me, the writer — adding to the young writer's repertoire of starting sounds. (Show children that a vowel can have several sounds. Later, when formal spelling training begins in second grade, teach them the rules governing those alternative sounds.)

If you consider what letters young writers need to write, you will see that teaching the letters of the alphabet starting at **A** and going to **Z** is not the most useful approach.

Upper case and lower case: Added to the difficulty of matching language sounds to a symbol is the fact that these symbols can be written in two ways; in capitals and small letters. The lower-case letters should come first. Make capital letters special. Tell youngsters, *We use a special letter to start our names.* And later: *We use the special capital letters to start our sentences.* This concept will come in handy when you teach capitalization through editing.

Dictation

Use dictation to demonstrate the connection between oral and written language, to demonstrate the concept of symbols conveying a message, to show the one-to-one correspondence of words to message, to show print directionality, text wrapping, and finger spaces.

You will not have time in daily writing workshop to take dictation from any one child more than once every few days. In the remaining sessions, the child is on his own. He may ask other children for help, using the Help Strip or designated helpers.

Emergent writers in the first three stages — Picture Writer, Verbal Storyteller, and Letter Copier — will need to see their messages written by you. Their inner words, words that have significance to them, should be the ones you additionally write on cards for them to create a word bank that they can carry, memorize, read to other children, and copy to their papers. Punch a hole in the corner of each card. Help children put their cards on a key-chain ring, shower curtain clip, or such.

Perfect your block printing and practice writing fast. Use the following technique when you take children's dictation to maximize the modeling benefit from the procedure. The technique can be used with physically handicapped students and illiterate adult students as well.

Dictation technique

1. Place the child on the opposite side from your pencil hand. She must be able to see your pencil point forming the letters. Hold the paper at an angle for the child to see both your hand and the writing as you work.
2. Ask the child to say what she wants you to write. Repeat it back to her.
3. Write in lower-case manuscript except when capitalization is appropriate
4. Write the message exactly the way the child says it. If a sentence is grammatically incorrect, you should tell the child the correct way to say it. Then ask the child how she would like you to write it.
5. Write each word slowly, pronouncing each word as you write, particularly stressing the beginning sound.
6. Stop often and have the child read the message back with you.
7. Point with your finger to each word as the child reads it with you.
8. Help the child trace the letters of the message with a pencil.
9. Encourage the child to read her message to other writers.

Write a word-bank card during some dictation sessions. Print the child's key message word, the content word, on a card for her word bank. *I like pizza. It's good.* The content word is *pizza*.

Sentence strips

Using the same dictation technique, write a child's message on a strip of card stock. Leave room on the strip for the child to write the sentences below your writing. Have child trace over your letters first. Then have him write the sentences below yours. Children should read their sentence strips to other children and keep them on a ring or clipped together in a manila envelope.

Inventory

Show children how to make lists of words that start with the same sound. Publish class collections of starting letters and words that start with them. Invite young writers to contribute a page. With children's input, make class charts of word families and repetitive phrases. These activities demonstrate several print principles: Flexibility Principle — child experiments with letters: reverses, writes upside down, and discovers conventionality of letter symbols; Inventorying Principle — child lists what he knows: letters, words, phrases, etc.; Recurring Principle — child repetitively uses groups of words for competence and confidence: *I like..., I have a..., I can...*; Generating Principle — child starts to create his own text from known elements.

Nancy Irwin, Abel Elementary, Bradenton, FL, introduces her first graders to the consonant blends: gr, br, dr, tr, cr, fr, and pr by reading picture books to them about grandfathers, brothers, dragons, trees, crabs, frogs, and praying mantises. After making charts of words that begin with those blends, she models using them in daily-writing-workshop starting components (a brother informational piece, a grandfather personal narrative, a dragon story, etc.). Then, her children dictate or write their own blend-word pieces in little folded paper booklets. One of her children, a science whiz, wrote about birds of prey, prairie dogs, and predators, getting the content words from a Ranger Rick magazine article.

Copying

Encourage the earliest emergent writers (Stages Two and Three) to copy the text of well-illustrated picture books that have only a word or two on each page. Read the books to the children before they start. Make small folded-paper booklets for the activity.

Innovation

Use textless picture books for the Picture Writer (Stage One) and the Verbal Informer (Stage Two). Invite them to tell about the pictures and take dictation from them when they do. The more advanced writers of Stages Five through Seven can write text for the books themselves — in consonant strings, repetitive phrases, or sentences. Again, provide folded-paper booklets, or separate half-page papers that they can put beside the book page as they work. Clip their half-page papers together for a small book when they finish.

Sight Words from Daily Environment

Collect packages, advertisements, pictures (or photos) of street signs, etc. — words children see every day. Have children collect them, as well. In a group session, have children read their packages and pictures. Help children cut out the words (retaining enough of the background to remember the context) and paste them on cards. Punch holes in the corners of the cards and put them on their key rings. Invite children to read these to each other and to use them in their writing.

Model: Show children a card with the word MILK, cut from a container, pasted on it. Write a sentence as you say it aloud: I like to drink MILK. Yum, yum.

Personal Writing

Start your daily writing workshop often with modeled writing about personal expertise or personal experiences. Your model will consist of drawing, labeling, and writing a message about the drawing. Always write more than one sentence. You will use the model to demonstrate left-to-right direction, finger spaces, consonant string writing, wrapping of printed text, consistency of small letters in printing, capitalizing the word 'I' and names, using end punctuation, etc.

Your Model: Put a tab on this page to help you find it quickly when you are ready to use it.

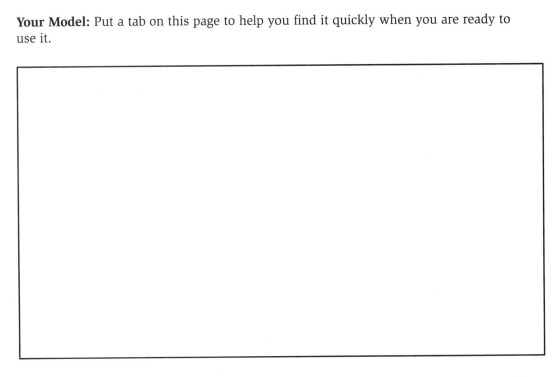

And More: Prepare a set of four to six personal expository and narrative pieces you will use for the models you present at the start of writing workshops or in group lessons. Use these prepared models until modeling becomes natural and easy for you. Children love to hear, again and again, the information and stories you write. So do not worry that you have used a model previously. They love hearing what you think and what you know. Children respect knowledge. Favorite teachers are loved for their knowledge and stories. Think back to your favorite teachers.

Additional Opportunities for Daily Writing

Once your daily writing workshop is established, you will find many opportunities to incorporate writing throughout the day and across the curriculum. Here are some examples that have proven effective.

The Morning Message

In Nancy Irwin's first-grade class, two students compose the morning message on a portable white dry-marker board and present it to the class at 9:30 a.m. Nancy modeled this activity during the first month of school. Then, student partners take over.

The two students have 15-20 minutes to compose and prepare the message. They are armed with a laminated list of the activities for each day and teachers' names for specials. Nancy tells the message makers about specific things that need to be included. They are responsible for finding the day and date, and for describing the weather.

Nancy uses the message for a brief lesson about phonics, numbers, editing, or anything else that arises from the content of the message. For example, if the month is May, she might ask children for all the rhyming words for May: day, say, hay, bay, lay, ray, pay, Jay.

Homework Writing

Writing homework is a way to ensure daily composing. It is also a way to show parents what their children are learning in daily writing workshop. Some schools ask parents and children to sign a contract that explains their responsibilities for homework writing. Here are several examples of homework writing.

- A kindergarten class mascot goes home each night. The child who takes it home tells what happened to the mascot while it was visiting her house and writes about that in writing workshop.
- Children take a Writer's Kit home to make a book with an adult or older sibling. They read their books in class the next day during a sharing time.
- Children keep a homework writing journal. Be sure to write a target skill on a page of their journal before they take it home. Review the target skill for the homework writing. Example: *Tonight, in your writing, use a number word — one, three, ten, a billion* (see Chapter 11). Students may paste a picture on the page and try to use the target skill as they write about the picture. *Two cats are in a box. One is looking out.* They may show their parents how they use a target skill in their writing or they can ask for help in using the target skill. Respond to the children's journals on a rotational basis, complimenting young writers on their use of target skills.

Science Journaling

In science work, where observation and description are part of the project, assign a writing target skill for each observation.

For instance, if your first-grade class is studying meal worms in a life-cycle project, students will make observations in a prepared folded-paper journal. For each observation, assign a writing target skill that must be incorporated into the observation. One might be to use a color word — *My meal worms are brown. They aren't moving.* Or, a comparison in description — *My meal worm are longer than a seed. One is bigger than the other.* Or, the use of a question mark — *Is my meal worm dead? I think it is.*

Entries in Class Logs and Charts

Marilyn Cafaro, Gulf Gate Elementary, Sarasota, FL, places a journal next to the classroom pet cage or tank. She invites her first- and second-grade students to sit for five minutes during free time, observe the pet, stamp the date on a page, and say something. She reminds them to write neatly because other children will be reading the log. Students read selections aloud from the log periodically. This is a composing activity that is useful at all grade levels, particularly in support of science-skill development in observation and description.

Summary

Do not confuse copying from the board with writing. While this may help children with the mechanical part of writing, it is not composing. Nor, is handwriting practice composing. The writing component of daily writing workshop must be devoted to children composing. They will imitate and use the lessons from your models. They will write about what they see, know, think, imagine, and remember.

Chapter 7
Response

Young children love to share their pieces, and they should read them to as many other writers as possible. Author's Chair, peer conferences, and sharing with the teacher during the daily writing workshop provide the response mechanisms young writers need. When they hear their writing and get a positive response — a compliment or a comment — they are encouraged to write again. When they hear their own work and their peers respond to it, they often add to what they said. In addition, these classroom response mechanisms provide opportunities to integrate the four language arts: reading, writing, talking, and listening.

Model each of the response mechanisms described in the following pages, for your young writers. In so doing, you will learn the kinds of compliments, comments, and encouragement that young writers need to thrive.

Do not be concerned about the amount of revision primary students generate from the responses they receive. It will be small. The objective of this writing-process stage, *response*, is for young writers to hear their own writing and to realize they have an audience for it. This realization will lead to a conscious consideration for their readers as they mature as writers.

Author's Chair

Author's Chair is the main response mechanism in a primary writing workshop. It gives children a chance to hear themselves and an opportunity for you to teach or reinforce writing skills. Through its use, you will foster a sense of ownership and authorship in young writers and a sense of a community in the classroom.

Author's Chair is used to a greater extent in the primary grades, where writers' manuscripts are relatively short, than in classes of older students, where manuscripts are longer. In the primary grades, you can conduct Author's Chair for 3-6 children at a sitting.

After your informal, initial use of Author's Chair during the first few days of school and writer's workshop (described in Chapter 2), model Author's Chair as it will be conducted during the rest of the year. You will model the language of compliments, comments, and questions.

Attendance: When writing time is an established routine, children need not attend every Author's Chair. If you are using Author's Chair for a lesson, call together those children who are working on the skill you plan to illustrate. If you are using Author's Chair for sharing, and some children are absorbed in their writing, do not interrupt them. Later, describe and practice how students can quietly join an ongoing Author's Chair or class meeting.

For a quiet signal to start Author's Chair, you might sit beside the chair and say to writers nearby: *I need an audience.* And, *Thank you, Merrill; Thank you, Mike; Thank you, Colby,* as the children take their places. Have children lay their papers on the floor in front of them. Children do not bring pencils to Author's Chair.

Record Keeping: Be sure to keep records of who has had a turn and make sure every child gets a chance to be in Author's Chair.

I would not recommend conducting Author's Chair for more than six writers at any given sitting. The rest of the children will usually become restless and stop listening. Show them that you are keeping track of who has had a turn in Author's Chair and who will get to go next time. They will learn to wait their turn if you adhere to the rotation.

When the Author Reads a Manuscript: *Do not hold the writer's paper.* Place your chair to the side of Author's Chair and slightly behind it. Help authors if they request it.

Writers may ask their partners to read their pieces. They may ask you, too. You may read the piece for a writer, but do not make a habit of it. When you do, ask the writer to stand at your side and help you with parts you can not read. Turn and whisper to the writer often, *What is this part of the picture? What is this word?* This way they are involved, in spite of themselves.

If writers are not ready to read in front of their classmates, do not call on them. Some writers may take several weeks before they feel confident enough to share. Once they see that Author's Chair is safe, most children will readily volunteer.

Modeling Author's Chair

When writers share their work in Author's Chair, their audience needs to respond in several ways. First, listeners must demonstrate that they heard the piece and understand what it is about. Secondly, they should be prepared to compliment the writer. Here is a description of how to conduct Author's Chair for maximum benefit to all your young writers.

For each model, you will need
- a clipboard holding your class list in table-form to check off Author Chair attendance by date — The list should have a larger column to write brief notes.
- small adhesive labels: smiley faces, stars, birds, flowers, colored file labels
- two to four articulate children and their writing work of that day **(Reminder: whenever you model, choose your participants carefully. The model needs to go smoothly and predictably.)**
- (optional, but desirable) — a microphone and amplification system — Portable cassette tape players often accept a microphone jack.

Receiving a Writer's Work

The foremost task of the Author's Chair audience is to hear and react to the author's piece. Listeners need to focus on the topic, the content. They need to assure a young writer that they heard what she wrote and that they can relate to it.

A. Gather the class together at the end of a writing session. Have children bring their writing to the meeting. Tell them you are going to show some of the things they will be doing at Author's Chair.

B. Tell them that a writer is going to share her work and that some of them will repeat what they heard.

C. Have one of the four pre-selected writers read her piece. Call on two children, in turn, to tell what they heard. Thank them.

D. Now, ask the writer to repeat her piece and model a statement that shows you *connect* to the writer's topic, such as:
    I have a dog, too.
    My mom looks like your mom.
    I wish I had a dog like yours.
    Does your dog lick your face like mine does?
    I had a toy car like that when I was little.
    My house has a chimney, too.

E. Invite your students to say something to the writer as you did. Entertain anything. Youngsters will not be good at this at first.

F. Repeat the same procedure with your next two or three authors.

G. Now, invite all the children to share their writing with a partner. Tell them to repeat what they hear and say something that shows they can connect to the author's topic. Tell them you will be asking listeners what their partner wrote when they finish. Send several pairs to the periphery of the room to disperse their voices.

H. After a few minutes, re-assemble, quiet the group, and ask, *Who would like to tell what their partners wrote?* Hear several volunteers.

I. Thank all the writers and tell them they will have a chance to do this again tomorrow, at the end of writing time.

J. Record the names of students who shared in Author's Chair. Make notes after their names of anything you observed in their writing: use of finger spaces; elements in their drawing; labeling; symbols. These dated notes will support your progress reports to parents.

Giving a Compliment

After several weeks of writing workshop, introduce this second model of Author's Chair to your writers. Explain that authors need to know what readers think of their writing. Tell your students about how you ask a colleague to respond to your rough drafts of letters home to parents, presentations you may make at meetings, or reports to the principal.

A. Gather the class to Author's Chair. Pre-select two writers to use in the model.

B. Explain to the children that there is another way they can help a writer in Author's Chair besides proving they listened. Talk about compliments. Give several to your students: *I like the way you came and sat down quietly for our class meeting. I like the way you put your knapsacks away this morning. I saw you pick up Vanessa's paper and give it to her. That was polite of you.*

C. Tell children they will be giving compliments to writers. Write the word, **compliment**, on the easel or board. Hand a child a card with **compliment** printed on it to add to the word-bank wall.

D. Ask the first writer to read his piece. Remind children to use their playground voices in Author's Chair so everyone can hear.

E. Ask someone to tell what she heard. Ask someone to connect to the writer's topic, reviewing the previously modeled responses.

F. Now, model some compliments. Find as many as you can. When you give the compliment, place one of the labels on the writing at the very place you compliment the author. Compliment anything. (Some children call these stickers **Did-It Dots,** when they identify and compliment target-skill use in their peer conferences.)

I like the way you made the sun.
I like the color you used.
I like the way you told about your sister.
I like the way you labeled the house, H.
I like the way you told about your toys.
I like that T.
I like the way you read your piece.

> Giving compliment stickers in this model is another example of using concrete aids in a writing-process activity — a very important principle to follow in teaching elementary children.

G. Before calling the second writer to Author's Chair, ask the first writer how it felt to share the piece and hear the compliments. Thank the first writer.

H. Invite the second writer to read her piece. When she finishes, ask your young writers to repeat what she wrote, react to it, or give a compliment. If a child has a compliment, give him a sticker to put on the writer's paper near the information or words he compliments.

I. Typical first reactions will tend to be general and not reflect listener engagement with the piece. *It was good. That was good writing. That's a good picture.* Such comments are not useful to a writer. Invite the responders to pick out exactly what they liked. Use the word, *specific.* Give a specific example yourself.

   I liked it when you said "crashed and smashed." They were great action words.
   I like how you used finger spaces.
   I liked it when you said the dog was "as big as a pony."
   I could really picture it when you told about your sister.
   The most beautiful word I heard was "pounce." (Ask children what was the most beautiful word they heard when you read aloud to them as well. Develop their ear for vocabulary and develop their love of words and language.)

J. When a young student gives a specific compliment, write it on your clipboard along with the responder's name. Tell the class what you are doing, thereby letting them know that you think their response is important. Compliment the children who gave a good compliment.

K. Read back the good compliments you entered on your clipboard. Tell the class you will make a chart of these compliments for all to see. Invite them to copy the ones they like on a card and bring them to the next Author's Chair.

L. The main goal of this model it to achieve specificity of compliments. Author's Chair participants, both the writers and the listeners, think about the things they hear complimented. They will begin to add them to their own writing. Often, they will use them incorrectly or illogically. That's all right. They are willing to take a risk. They will learn by their mistakes.

Thumbs-up for the Target Skill

In a later Author's Chair session, following the introduction of target skills through picture-prompted writing, show children how they can give a silent thumbs-up signal when they hear the author hit one of the skills under study. (See Chapter 11 for target skills.)

Focus on Vocabulary

What word did you hear the writer use that you just love? Have children listen for favorite words. When a peer compliments a writer on words he used, the community thrives.

A writer's partner liked the word — tennis.

Summary

Keep the first models of Author's Chair simple and limited to listening, reaction, and compliments. Compliments validate a student's work and himself. The ability of students to compliment each other's work and to celebrate each other's accomplishments is a very important aspect of a writing community.

Repeat the Author's Chair models several times during the year, emphasizing the areas of greatest need. Author's Chair serves also as a model for peer conferencing. The same listener responses apply.

Results of an Effective Author's Chair

- Young writers know that others value what they have to say.
- Writers have an opportunity to hear their own work.
- Students know what everyone else is writing.
- Students practice attentive listening.
- Students hear new words.
- Writers are complimented for the things they do well. (Rewarded behavior is repeated behavior.)
- Writers see how the techniques they hear used and complimented might apply to their own writing.
- Writers find mistakes when they hear themselves read their manuscripts.
- The sense of community is reinforced.
- You have the opportunity to give brief, on-the-spot lessons.
- You can record evidence of an emergent writer's progress.
- You hear the application of skills you have been teaching.
- You have laid the foundation for the transition to peer conferencing.

Peer Conferences

In kindergarten all year, and at the start of the year in first grade, Author's Chair is the primary mechanism for sharing and responses. Since manuscripts are relatively short, as many as six writers can experience this mode of sharing at the end of most writing periods.

But, as your classroom writing community develops, young writers' manuscripts will grow in length and complexity. Author's-Chair time may accommodate only two or three writers. You can not hear all their work during writing workshop. When your class reaches this point, you will want to develop effective peer conferencing to satisfy young writers' need for response. Even emergent writers in the first three stages, who can not read their own writing, can take part in peer conferencing, acting as listeners and responders.

Peer conferencing, in fact, will come to replace Author's Chair as the main response mechanism in daily writing workshop. As with Author's chair, you must model peer conferences if you want them to work. Peer partners must know exactly what their jobs are and exactly what is the purpose of the conference. The most efficient peer conferences involve a narrow focus or a single specific task.

Do not expect young writers to critique and correct each other's manuscripts in peer conferences. Do, however, show them how to compliment each other for using a target skill and how to help each other use a target skill when they have not. The first peer conferences for young writers should be limited to identifying and complimenting target skill use. Later, as students become adept at peer conferencing, or if you have a class with previous experience in it, model conferences that include questions and comments that cover a larger range of writing considerations.

When and Where Children Peer Conference

Young writers peer conference during the writing and sharing components of daily writing workshop. They conference informally as they write. Writing partners often talk as they compose; checking on what each other is doing or discussing the target skill for the piece. Encourage children to stop periodically as they write and read to their partners what they have written.(Remind them to use "murmur voices".)

You can designate a specific place in the room for those writers who have finished their writing to peer conference. They meet there with pre-arranged peer partners, or with the next writer who is finished. Writers can indicate when they are ready by going to the area — in front of the easel, at a table, in a corner. Some teachers have children place a clothespin, with their name printed on it, on a square or circle of oak tag labeled Peer Conferencing. This helps you keep track of what young writers are doing while you rove to encourage, work with a group, or conference.

Modeling Knee-to-Knee Conferences

As with all workshop procedures, use these models early in the year. Although they take time, they pave the way for more productive writing sessions during the rest of the year.

Young writers should be introduced to peer conferencing called *Knee-to-Knee* as early as kindergarten. In Knee-to-Knee, two students move their chairs to face each other and sit with knees almost touching. This encourages keen listening.

Carol Collins, Palmetto Elementary, Palmetto, FL, introduces the model when most of her first graders can read back what they have just completed or can read what they wrote the day before. Her students regularly write in spiral-bound journal notebooks. They will do one or two knee-to-knee peer conferences per week.

The Knee-to-Knee model is presented in a series of steps, with each succeeding step requiring a new response from the peer partners. Build this progression during the first two months of writing workshop. Model each step separately. When your students have mastered the first response, introduce the next one. As they conference, have peer partners use the successive steps you have modeled. The listeners' responses are similar to those you modeled for Author's Chair.

1. **Receiving the piece.** Responder: *You said you have cows and you help your dad.*
2. **Reacting to the content.** Responder: *I know lots of stuff about cows.*
3. **Complimenting target-skill use.** Responder: *You said "milking" and that's an action word.*
4. **Making comments or asking questions:** Responder: *Do cows sleep?*

The writer can prompt his peer partner with such questions as: *What else would you like to know? Can you picture this?*

As discussed earlier in the Author's-Chair model, children will tend to give general compliments. Model compliments again and again to help peer partners be more specific. Use the word *specificity* often. The children in Carol Collins' class brainstorm lists of specific compliments and useful questions. These are placed on charts for the students to use during writing workshop.

I recommend using **label stickers** in the peer conferences when children compliment each other's skill use. Model how to give a compliment sticker.

- The listener draws a star or smiley face, or the letter standing for the target skill on the sticker — C for color word, N for number, F for feeling, BJV for big, juicy verb, C for comparison, L for list, Q for question, H for hook, etc. Using initials reinforces the concept of letters standing for messages, an important concept for emergent writers to learn.
- The listener places the sticker on the manuscript right where the writer used the target skill.
- If the writer did not hit the target, his peer partner puts the sticker in the upper right corner with his own initials near it. By checking papers for the stickers at the top right corner, you can quickly determine which writers could not use the target skill. You can then schedule a group lesson with those writers to review the skill.

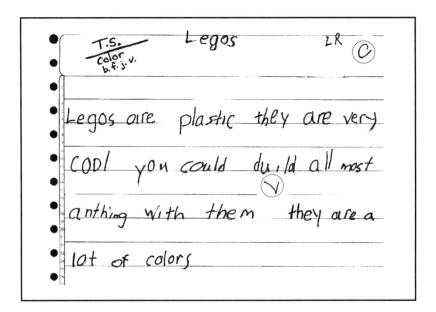

Selecting Peer Partners

To start, peer pairs may be students sitting in adjacent desks. As you learn more about your young writers, you might assign partnerships for a specific length of time. As children become proficient with *Knee-to-Knee*, they will begin to request particular partners. If these partnerships result in better writing, accommodate them. Remind children that best friends are not always the best peer partners. Best friends will say, *That's great. I like it.* That's what best friends are for. But, for writing response, you want a good listener, someone who writes about the same things as you, a writer who can help you with the target skill.

Some Results of Modeling a Peer Conference

- Writers get to hear and share their writing. This builds a sense of authorship and ownership.
- Writers understand what their job is in a peer conference and that they do not have to correct each other's paper.
- Students acquire a supply of basic compliments, comments, and questions to use in their own conferences.

Sharing Writing

The Rules for Sharing Examples During a Lesson

It is as important for young writers to share their attempts and failures, as it is their successes. When students try out a writing technique during a lesson or model, always call on a few volunteers to share early into the writing — as soon as you see some students have written a few words or a sentence. This will help the non-starters who may not know what to do, have difficulty processing oral directions, missed the directions, or need to know *what is the right way, what is acceptable* before they start. In addition, it helps the children who wrote by validating what they have done.

Sharing during writing time should be modeled and its rules adhered to. These rules should be published as well as reiterated often:

- **Anyone who is in the middle of a thought and is writing it should continue to write.** Be sure to let students know that capturing their thoughts takes priority over listening to a share. You might turn to the volunteer sharer in the model and ask, *Do you see that Jason is continuing to write? Is he disturbing you? Are you satisfied with half the class listening while you share?*
- **Anyone who is between thoughts should listen to the volunteer who is sharing.**
- **No one may talk during a volunteer's recital.** Remind the students who have continued to write during the sharing that they may join in listening whenever they care to.

These rules promote and respect important aspects of a daily writing workshop: community, continuity, and the chance to become absorbed in writing.

Sharing at the End of Writing Workshop

In addition to conducting an Author's Chair and having children read their writing to one other person before putting it away, there are other ways to provide for sharing.

- **Try Speedy Vertical Author's Chair.** Gather your students to the meeting area as soon as they have finished writing. Ask them to remain standing while you call on one student to read his piece. When the author finishes, call on a child who has raised her hand to tell what the piece was about. Next, invite that responder to read her piece, and call on a new responder to tell what that piece was about, and so on.

Continue this speedy response activity until half the class has had a turn. This rapid Author's-Chair chain helps broadcast topics to your writing community and provides the opportunity for writers to hear their writing again. It is conducted standing, purely for the sake of giving the children a chance to stretch after writing. Record who read and who responded on a class-list check sheet.

- **Use Recordings for Audio Portfolios.** Provide each first-grade student with a blank tape in the middle of the year. Show the students how to use the class tape recorder. Have them select their best piece and practice reading it to a peer. Schedule time for them to record the piece on their own tape.

  Keep the tape in the student's portfolio. Make these tapes available for parent conferences, perhaps setting up a listening station in the hall where parents who are waiting for conferences can hear their child's tape.

Individual Student/Teacher Conferences

What is the Major Objective of a Student/Teacher Conference?

Think of a writing conference as a time to learn what stage an emergent writer is in, to learn what a student writes about, to react to his content, and to encourage him with a compliment, comment, or guidance. With practice, this can take very little time.

You should not anticipate a conference as an opportunity to locate and correct all the mistakes a writer has made. Most of a child's writing should be viewed as practice, not as a finished product. As is true for any skill or craft, writers have to write badly before they write well. By focusing on the things writers do well, you encourage them to write again.

All young writers want their teacher to read or hear their work. They pull and tug at your sleeve, talk while you are trying to hear someone else, wave their papers about. *Listen to this. Wait, I want to read this to you. Listen to me. I wrote about my cat.*

It is difficult to hear everyone. Teachers become discouraged when they can't respond to all their students. They see work go unfinished because writers couldn't get a response when they needed one.

Though it may not be possible to conference for ten minutes with each of your young writers on each of their manuscripts, it is possible, *and important*, to respond to all your writers and to provide continual encouragement and guidance. You need to recognize *any one-on-one exchange between a writer and the teacher* as a conference. That means the following qualify as conferences.

- Author's Chair: your comments or questions
- roving conferences
- group lessons
- short, prepared conferences with individual writers
- comments made to a writer on the playground, in the hall, in passing

The following are some ways to help you conference with young writers.

Cue Card

Prepare a cue card to carry on your roving conferences. This will speed things up. On it, write the comments and questions you intend to ask writers. Some may be suitable for a specific genre, others may be general. As you become facile with conferences, you will probably dispense with the cue card and rely on knowledge about your students and their writing to guide the conference. But it is a great help in the early days of daily writing workshop.

Some Positive Things to Do or Say. Receive the content, tell it back, enjoy it, relate to it.
- I see you hit the target and used...
- I like the way you have...
- I can really picture...
- This is easy for me to read.
- How did you learn that?
- I do the same thing...
- Tell me again what happened. Did you put it down that way?
- What else do you want your reader to know?
- How did you select this topic?
- I see you have included some content words of this topic.

Some Things Not to Do or Say
- Don't take control of the piece by interjecting your ideas or by soliciting information that takes the piece in a direction you think it should go.

- Avoid — *I think you should..., Don't you want to tell...? Here's a place you could...*

Group Conferences

A small-group conference (four writers maximum) works well in first grade. As you receive, compliment, and comment on a writer's piece, the other two or three children can be invited to make compliments, identify target-skill use, and ask questions, too. As they listen to your conference comments and interaction with the writer, they learn what a conference is all about, they hear lessons reiterated, they learn what other writers are doing.

Give the writer whose turn it is, the dominant place in the seating arrangement. Explain to the other children that your attention will be on the writer and his work. Give them their task: identify target-skill "bull's eyes" with a silent thumbs-up. (Skip stickers in this conference format as it will slow the process down. Invite them to meet privately with the author afterward to give stickers.)

Short Individual Conferences

Conduct individual conferences during rest time or during the writing component of daily writing workshop. Schedule them anytime throughout the day when you can work with individual children.

In kindergarten, this is an opportunity to take dictation for young writers who have not broken the sound-to-symbol code. Ask these writers to tell you about their drawing. Write what they tell you in lower case letters that they can then trace over. (See the Dictation Model in Chapter 6.) Start with one word, one phrase, or one sentence of dictation depending on a child's abilities and concentration span.

For writers who have made the sound-to-symbol connection, conduct a conference based on encouragement and providing information to move them from single-consonant writing to full sentences.

Preparation for the conference:
- Look at the child's piece before the conference.
- Record anecdotal notes about growth and achievement.
- Prepare a comment about the content.

- Prepare a response that focuses on all the good things the writer has done.
- Select *one* major area in writing development to discuss with the writer that will help her progress.

Conferences should offer a writer *encouragement* and a reaction to the content and presentation of her piece. The most difficult thing in conferencing is curbing the temptation to correct all the things you see wrong with the student's writing. You must content yourself with addressing just one need. Attention to any more can easily overwhelm and discourage a young writer. You can note and record other areas in which the writer needs help and use this information for lesson planning and future conferences.

Chapter 8
Revision

Response and revision go together like peanut butter and jelly. Revision is what a writer does to his piece when his readers say they don't understand it or there isn't enough to it to make it interesting. In classroom writing workshops, young writers get these responses from their peers and their teacher.

Revision is not the same thing as editing. In revision, the writer is concerned that his message is clear and interesting. In editing (proofreading), the writer is preparing the message for public consumption and is concerned with writing conventions. Be careful not to call correcting spelling or punctuation errors, and such, revision.

Young writers are not naturally inclined to revise, particularly if they are led to believe that revision is a correction of something wrong. They should be encouraged to view revision as making something good, better. *Good is best's worst enemy.* (Ultimately, the quality of a piece of writing is determined by the amount of revision a writer is willing to do.) Revision, looking at a piece of writing again with an eye to improving it, should be introduced in the primary grades and developed in later grades.

Young writers will revise if three conditions are satisfied: if you model revision techniques, if you provide ample opportunity for them to share and get responses to their writing, and if they have room on their paper.

But, do not force revision. Do not make it a prerequisite to publishing in the primary grades. Make it a natural part of the writing process by modeling it and using appealing language: *You might need to do some Band-Aid work here; Just paste another line on the bottom; No problem, just add some more here; What a neat way you added the target skill.*

Kinds of Revision Primary Writers Do

Addition

The revision most emergent writers can do is additive. Those in the first three writing stages can do it orally. When these children share their pictures with you, or when you take dictation, encourage them to tell more about their drawing. When they see revision models directed to advanced writers, and see that revision is something writers do, they will begin to add more marks or color to their paper or another element to their drawing.

Writers in later stages may add elements to their drawing, another label to their pictures, another letter to their letter strings, another item to their lists, or another word or sentence to their pieces. Demonstrate all these kinds of revision in your modeled writing. Show young writers how to add details to both their drawings and writing.

When young writers add more information, do not expect that they will add it in a logical fashion. They will add words or sentences at the end, with no thought to logic or sequence. (Show them how to add more paper to their manuscript by taping or stapling to accommodate their revision.) Young writers do not add gracefully or logically to their work until late third or early fourth grade.

Substitution and Deletion

Young writers find it harder to make *substitutions* than *additions*. Firstgraders, following your models, can begin to substitute specific nouns for general nouns — *oatmeal* for *cereal*, or *KMart* for *store*. They can substitute livelier verbs for dull ones — *gobbled* for *ate*.

When young writers in late first grade or second grade begin to write narratives, they will often use the phrase *And then* repetitively. They say *And then* when they tell you stories. It's their way of keeping you as an audience. Lessons about replacing repetitive *And thens* with time orienters is appropriate for these children. (See Chapter 14 for a lesson about replacing *And then* with narrative time transitions.)

Young writers find *deletions* harder still. Actually, all writers find deletion difficult. *What? I have to take out that word, that sentence? It's my favorite part!* But, through reading their writing to a partner, some young writers may find a word written twice and delete it. Occasionally a child will find a sentence in an informational piece that is completely off the topic and see that it needs to be cut. These are rare and wonderful occurrences; treasure them. But, do not plan your writing program around them.

Reorganization

Emergent writers can not reorganize their writing. Reorganization is the most difficult revision task for all writers. It requires abstract thinking and a great deal of writing experience.

Some first graders do learn to combine short sentences using the word *and*. And, they can physically move sentence strips in their informational pieces during the sorting process. (See Precursor to Paragraphing in Chapter 13 for this lesson.)

How to Help Young Writers Revise

Modeling Revision

Start a writing workshop with modeled writing to show your young writers how to use the caret, ^. Draw a picture and write your message under it. As you write, say it.

My dog likes pizza. So do I.

Read your message back and say to your students, *I think I would like to add that he likes pepperoni best. That's really specific; my readers would like that. Some of them might like pepperoni pizza best, too. I can add that to my writing. Here's how authors do it. They put a little arrow point — it looks like a roof — where the word should go. It is called a caret. Then, they write the word up in the space above it. That shows you to go up and get that word while you are reading the sentence. Like this:*

       pepperoni
My dog likes ^ pizza. So do I.

Invite your students to try one. Write *I have a pet*, on the lower half of the blackboard or on a sheet of easel paper.

How many of you have a pet? How can we be more specific? A big pet, a pet mouse? Call on students who want to contribute a word. *Who would like to add to the pet sentence using a caret?* Invite a student to tell you what word to write, or to come up and write the word herself.

Bring out a prepared sheet of chart paper with the pet sentence written 10-15 times. Place it on the easel or hang it on the board. Tell writers they may add a ^ and their word to this class chart during writing workshop.

Invite your writers to try using the ^ when they write that day. Praise attempts and achievement alike during the sharing component.

Room on Their Paper

Young writers can't revise if there is no room on their manuscripts to do it. Ask any fourth- or fifth-grade teacher about their students' papers: solid, line after line of small cursive writing. It's next to impossible to get them to mess up their papers with revisions. So establish the habit of skipping lines in the primary grades.

Use greenbar accounting paper in daily writing workshop for later-stage emergent writers who are ready for lined paper. Tell your students to write on just one line, the white or the green (blue, in some cases) — their choice of course. This paper is just what they need to produce open manuscripts with room for revision.

Make Revision a Natural Part of the Writing Process

Revision it the key to good writing. It can be done best if the author puts his writing away for a time and later revisits it. For all writers, a rough draft is like road kill. The first day it doesn't smell so bad but leave it for a few days and it begins to stink. Young writers must have access to their stinky first drafts, the time and opportunity to return to them, and guidance about how to make them better.

Make a practice of having emergent writers in Stages Six and Seven, and your young developing writers, look at writing they did a week ago (entries in journals, work from their portfolios). Ask if they see something they did well. They can give themselves a sticker, or a draw a star. Ask them if they see where they may have left out a word. Can they add what goes there? Ask them if they can add more information, make something more specific, or use one of the target skills they have been practicing since they wrote the piece. Provide an ink stamp of the word REVISION or special stickers for them to indicate their additions or changes.

Revising to Target Skills

Encourage your young writers to read their work for target-skill use. They will do this as the object of peer conferencing and Author's Chair. You will need to show young writers how to hit-the-target if they miss it the first time through.

Model

Start a daily writing workshop with a lesson to show young writers how to add a target skill after a miss. For example, if the target skill was *using a comparison*, write the following on the easel or blackboard.

> *My cat is soft. She is white and black. I love her.*

Then say, *I forgot to make a comparison. Let me see. What else is soft, or black and white? My cat is soft as a...* (Pause here for children to supply some answers: a pillow, a cotton ball, my teddy bear.) *... I think I will put, as soft as a baby bunny.*

>   as   as a baby bunny
> *My cat is* ^ *soft* ^. *She is white and black. I love her.*

Continue: *My cat is white and black like a...* (Pause again for children to supply some comparisons: a zebra, a cow.) *Yes, I like that..., black and white like a cow.*

>   as   as a baby bunny   like a cow
> *My cat is* ^ *soft* ^. *She is white and black* ^. *I love her.*

Your model: Make up some sentences appropriate for some of the target skills you are teaching. Tab this page to find your model quickly. Later, make up sentences that cover as many target skills as you need for the year and keep them in your writer's notebook.

Combining Sentences

Combining sentences is one of the simplest forms of reorganization. You can model this for your first graders in the second half of the year.

Minilesson

Materials: five to eight sets of two or three small sentences ready for combining, written on index cards or small pieces of paper. Create several sets of small sentences beginning with the same word (*I like cats. I like big cats. I like small cats.*).

Procedure:
- Call the class or a group to the easel or board. If it is a small group, I usually have the children remain standing for a short lesson. They like the chance to learn in a different mode.

- Write several short sentences on the board.
  I have a dog. He is mean. He bites.
  I like pizza. I like cheese pizza. I like mushroom pizza.

- Ask the children to point to any sentences **that start with the same word or words**. In group one, *He is, He is*, and in the second, *I, I, I*. Remind them that authors avoid using the same word over and over and over. It puts the reader to sleep. (Remind your writers often about the concept of considering their readers.)

- Show the group how to combine little sentences that all start with the same words using the word *and*.
  I have a dog. He is mean and he bites.
  I like pizza with cheese and mushrooms.

- Write another set on the board. Ask for a volunteer to combine sentences, orally or by writing on the board.

- Give each child a set of small sentences beginning with the same word or phrase. Ask them to combine the sentences orally. Invite them to write them on the board as well.

- Finally, invite these students to work in a group, checking each other's *writing* for short sentences that start with the same word. If they find some praise them and help them combine the sentences with *and*.

Your model

Write several sets of simple sentences to use in your mini-lesson about combining sentences. Tab the page to find it quickly.

Young writers need to view their writing as something that is not over and done with in one sitting. They should leave the primary grades with this notion firmly established in their writing attitude.

Because primary-grade writers do not revise easily, and then, only by addition, limited substitution, and minor reorganization, we need to help them write as well as they can the first time through. We can do this by putting a premium on prewriting and by having them concentrate on using target skills when they write.

Chapter 9
Editing

How do I get my primary students to edit their writing? Am I doing too much? Should I expect them to be able to correct their spelling? Editing looms as a serious concern for most writing teachers. We remember how our school papers were edited by our teacher and think we must continue that tradition. The silly thing was that we would make all the corrections our teacher noted, re-copy it, take it home; and our parents thought we'd done it. Our teachers got to be good editors. We can teach students to become good editors. Here's how to do it:

- Teach the conventions of punctuation, capitalization, grammar, usage, and spelling through application. Make them the function of editing and the object of your class publishing standards. There is nothing wrong with practicing these skills using pre-printed practice sheets, as long as application remains the dominant mode.

- Set reasonable classroom editing-for-publishing standards. Tell parents or guardians what they are. Make sure they know about the editing procedures in your classroom.

- Teach children the principles of editing in daily writing workshop.

Publishing Standards

Not all writing in your classroom daily writing workshop needs to be edited and published. Most children's writing in the primary grades should be regarded as pure practice. Pieces that are published or placed in portfolios, however, do need to be edited.

Published pieces should be edited to conform to established standards. The standards will vary according to the conventions for which young writers can edit *independently*. If you want a perfect product, additional editing will be your responsibility, but is always done with the consent of the author.

The first **kindergarten** publishing standard, established half-way through the year, might be that all published work must
- have the author's name on it
- have the date stamped on it
- have a period at the end of all the scribbles, letter strings, words, or sentences

Later in the year, the standard might be that all published work must also
- have the word 'I' capitalized
- have a title

An initial **first-grade** publishing standard might be that a published work must
- have the author's name on it
- have 'I' capitalized
- itself start with a capital letter and end with a period
- have a title

Later in the year, the standard might require that the work also
- have *sentences* that start with capitals and end with periods
- have content words spelled correctly

Does this mean some published pieces will contain errors? Yes, it does. If you insist that *all* errors be eliminated before your students publish, and you take on the task of correcting everything, your young writers will lose their sense of ownership and control, and they may cease writing. This is too large a price to pay for the dubious value of a perfect product **at this young age**.

Disclaimer

When you display writing work that your children have edited independently, post a disclaimer with it. Advise the viewing audience: *Young writers have edited these papers independently for the following writing conventions* _____.

These are young students learning a difficult and creative craft. We cannot insist on perfection in their writing any more than we can insist of perfection in their art, music, and sports. In these activities, we comfortably allow them stray lines, wrong notes, and misplays. In a similar manner, we need to allow them a few misspellings and missing punctuation in their writing.

Remember that writing conventions and editing speak only to the readability of a piece and have nothing to do with it's quality, per se. A computer can edit text, but only people can create informative, graceful, elaborate writing. The latter skills must be the main focus of our writing instruction.

Parents and Editing

Parents need to hear about your writing program. They need to know that you are indeed teaching writing skills. They must be educated to *focus on the content and composing skills* displayed in their children's work. It is essential that they are informed about the editing and publishing standards in your classroom so they can put them in proper perspective. A letter, such as the following, may help them understand the developmental nature of writing and the need for them to take an encouraging and tolerant stance. (See also Chapter 17.)

> *Dear Parents,*
>
> *Your children are engaged in the writing process. As authors, they are gathering their thoughts, writing, revising, editing, and publishing. You, their audience and readers, need to bear with them as they learn this important craft. At this stage, their published work will not be perfect.*
>
> *But just as you can all enjoy a junior high school band concert with the occasional clarinet squeaks and misplaced trumpet toots, or a midget-league baseball game with a few booted balls and bad throws, so too can you enjoy these young authors' writing performance with the occasional temporary spelling or misplaced period.*
>
> *I do teach and require children to edit their papers for some conventions that they understand. In this marking period, published work will be edited independently by your child for the following conventions:*
> (List the editing standard for the period covered by this letter.)

Teaching Editing

Young writers must practice editing to become adept at the skill. In this section you will find models and procedures that will help them become competent editors in some basic conventions. These procedures are based on how writers work and on children's natural abilities and limitations. They include

- editing by ear for end punctuation and beginning capitalization of the next sentence
- editing someone else's writing
- editing for one convention at a time
- editing for misspelling — grade two

Editing by Ear

It is easier to *hear* where end punctuation belongs than to *see* where it belongs. Chomsky's research[1] in the 1950s tells us that children acquire the syntax of their native language in the early months of infancy; they are born with the ability to do so. By the time they reach school age, they understand the complexities and nuances of the language in which they have been raised. It is this understanding that makes editing by ear possible and effective.

Editing by Ear for Sentence End Punctuation and Beginning Capitalization

Have you ever seen Victor Borge, comedian-pianist, perform his oral-punctuation routine? He reads a short selection of prose, using an array of vocal sounds and accompanying hand gestures to indicate each of the punctuation marks required in the piece. Of course, the sounds are silly and the piece is over-loaded with punctuation to increase the hilarious possibilities.

This routine can be adapted as a model for editing by ear. Present it to young writers as early as kindergarten. Introduce the model when a group of your writers are writing a sentence or more, or when some are ready to publish their first pieces. Restrict the first exercise to only one type of end punctuation, namely, periods.

The model takes approximately 25 minutes. Repeat it several times during the first semester as a starting component to writing workshop.

You will need:
- a Big Book, of fiction or fact, that the children know well. (Select one limited to end punctuation of periods for kindergarten. Select one with question- and exclamation marks for first and second graders.)
- the Author's Chair
- an easel and a pointer
- a writer with work that includes two or more sentences
- pre-determined peer partnerships with assigned places to meet

a) Gather the class in front of the easel. Tell them you are going to show them how authors know where to put the periods at the end of their sentences. Tell them they will need to do that so other people can read their writing.

b) Ask the students to read *chorally* with you from the Big Book. Encourage them to do it with feeling. Read declarative sentences with a slight voice drop (exclamations with a rise in pitch and volume, questions with a rise and pause). As you reach the end of each sentence, point out the end punctuation. Tell children a period is like a stop sign for a car driver; it tells the reader to stop. Often, a student will point out that the next sentence starts with a capital letter. If none does, do so yourself.

c) Continue with the choral reading until you think a majority of the students get the connection between the end punctuation and the sound of their voices. With first and second graders, continue until you have covered the three types of end punctuation.

---

[1]Noam Chomsky, *Syntactic Structures* (Mouton, 1957)

d) Now take the Big Book from the easel, so that the students cannot see the text, and read it to them. Ask students to snap their fingers or cluck with their tongues when they hear the end of a sentence as you read to them. Invariably, students will cluck and snap at random for the novelty of it. Acknowledge that urge and invite them to practice the snap and cluck for a moment or two. Then quiet them and proceed.

e) Point out how your voice sounds when you reach question marks, periods, and exclamation marks. Children may suggest two new signal sounds for questions and exclamations. Great!

f) Read through the book with the children supplying the end punctuation.

g) Now, invite a young writer to read his piece to the class. A kindergarten class will listen just for the end of sentences, where the periods go. First and second graders will listen for questions and exclamations as well. They will make the agreed signal sounds. The writer may have a pencil with him to add end punctuation he may have left out.

You will observe that the writer usually reads with greater-than-usual feeling and will start to look up expectantly when he reaches the end of sentences, anticipating classmates' clucks or snaps. Remind the first-grade writer that if he adds some end punctuation in response to the signal, he should start the next sentence with a capital letter. (Kindergarten children use upper and lower case letters indiscriminately and usually are not ready for this reminder.)

h) Invite another young writer to read a manuscript. Repeat the procedure. Even if a writer has just one sentence, go through the procedure. Kindergarten children like to write a huge period when they hear the end of the sentence. That's fine.

i) Now invite all the writers in the class to try this kind of editing in peer partnerships or groups. Give your young writers a few moments to read their pieces to themselves so that they can read smoothly. Remind the class that the job of the reader is to read the piece with feeling. The job of the listener is to give the signal for end punctuation, and, in first grade, to ask if the writer started the following sentence with a capital letter.

j) Do not expect 100 percent accurately edited work. Many writers will have incomplete sentences and read them incorrectly. Their partners will not know what to do in this case. This is a trial-and-error session.

k) Rove around the class helping and encouraging the partnerships.

l) When most of the partnerships have finished, ask the writers to put their initials on the top of their partners' papers.

m) Ask children if they found any missing end punctuation. Ask in this fashion: *Who found places that they could clap or cluck?* not, *Who forgot to add a period?* Always place the emphasis on the positive, praising the listening editor. Invite students to share the sentence they heard and the missing end punctuation they told their partner it needed. Let your students know that it was great if they found any. *What good editors you are!*

n) Remind your young writers that they will have a chance to do this again. Ask them to think about end punctuation and capitals the next time they write.

Reading Support for Editing by Ear and the Concept of Sentence

Choral reading is a wonderful way to tune young writers' ears to the sound of sentences. Teach children to say the sentences of a Big Book they love and have memorized, using the correct inflection for a period, a question, and an exclamation. This will help them when they edit by ear for end punctuation.

Once children can read by themselves, they should be encouraged to read aloud with feeling. This must be modeled, of course.

Mary Ann Landrum, Manatee County, FL, uses a reading-aloud technique in her unique independent reading program to develop children's ear for sentences. **She calls it murmur reading**. Her primary class is divided into five groups for rotational purposes.

- On the first day of a group's cycle, the children select a book to read independently. They look at the pictures and read silently for the remainder of the session. Landrum maintains an extensive library of fiction and non-fiction books for emergent to fluent readers.
- On the second day, the children sit along the classroom walls or in a hall and **murmur read**. This means they mouth the words, murmuring them quietly.
- On the third day, they prepare a selection (of predetermined length) and practice reading it aloud with feeling (murmuring if they are at the class edge).
- On the fourth day, readers meet with their group in a circle and take turns reading their practiced selections aloud. Their peers grade their oral-reading-with-feeling Olympics-style — holding up number cards, 1-5.
- On the fifth day, members of the group confer individually with Landrum to discuss the book and read a selection to her.

Landrum reports that her children are especially good at editing-by-ear and writing in complete sentences, both by-products of **murmur reading**.

Primary-grade writers do not respond to formal lessons about such abstract concepts as subject and predicate. Instead, use daily writing workshop techniques such as talking in knee-to-knee prewriting conferences, editing by ear, using sentence strips for dictation and recording information to reinforce children's ability to hear complete sentences.

Is This the Way it Goes?

In conferences, read a child's paper back to her exactly as it is written. If it does not have end punctuation, read it monotone with no inflection or pauses for sentence endings. Ask, *Is this the way it goes?* Writers can tell where their sentences end. They will stop you and say, *No, it goes like this.* Show them where they have to help out their reader with punctuation.

Editing Someone Else's Writing

Writers, at all levels, find it easier to edit someone else's paper than their own. Given a long enough interval between the writing and the editing of their own manuscripts, mature writers might find many of their errors.

Young writers find it difficult to edit their own work while information or the story is still in their heads. You will notice that they ad-lib when they read the piece, adding missing words and punctuation they did not write.

When they hear or read another writer's unfamiliar piece, they find errors more readily. Spelling, punctuation, and capitalization conventions can be reinforced by having them edit other writer's papers. The editors will internalize the conventions and begin to use them in their own writing.

When one of Carol Collins' first graders wants her to hear a piece, she occasionally calls on another young writer to do the reading. The author stands at his classmate's elbow and may prompt him. He may even take the paper back to make corrections when the reader says the wrong word. Collins says this ploy helps young authors learn that their writing has to be legible; that their readers need to be able to figure out what the words are. It puts pressure on writers to write legibly and to pay some attention to conventions when they present their papers.

Editing For One Convention at a Time

Class-Edit Model

Select one convention appropriate to the grade and writing level. The easiest conventions for first graders is the *capitalization of 'I' and names*. Make transparencies of students' writings that include uncapitalized I and names. Use samples from another class or another year and cover the authors' names.

Lead the students through an edit of the projected or copied manuscript for capitalization. For each edit, writers must give the reason for their corrections. *It's a boy's name; It's the name of his dog; It's the word I.*

Group Edit with the Teacher

In first and second grades, after you have presented the editing-by-ear model, meet with a group of five or six writers who have several sentences of writing. Ask each writer to read his own paper so he can read it smoothly. Review the end punctuation conventions that can be checked by editing-by-ear — periods, question marks, sentence starting capitalization. Then, ask one student to read aloud while you make the sound signals for end punctuation. Ask the other writers to join you in finding the periods or question marks for the first writer and in giving the sound signals. Continue until all have had a chance to have their work edited.

Meet again with this group to teach them to edit by ear, or visually, for capitalization. Review what they know so far about capitalization: the word 'I', names of people, days of week, etc. Have them *listen* to one child's piece for those things they know need capitalizing. They should identify the reason for capitalizing a word they spot.

Again, have them listen to each other's pieces, or trade papers and *look* for words that need capitalization. When they edit, they should write in pencil over lower-case letters to capitalize them, or over upper-case letters to uncapitalize them. Do not use valuable time teaching young writers proof-marking symbols. Rather, devote that time to teaching editing.

Repeat group editing with these young writers to identify and spell content words. (See Spelling, this chapter.) Have them help each other find the correct spelling for the words in the classroom environment.

Start editing training with a new group. Use the first group members to help others in the class. By the end of first grade, young writers should know how to edit each other's papers for these few basic conventions.

Editing Board

Review the conventions you want young writers to practice in their editing work. List these and other target skills for the current piece on the board, at a height where children can write their initials beside them. Ask students who are ready for the editing stage to form pairs and edit each other's papers for these items. Ask them to put their first names on the blackboard after each item as they accomplish it.

Capitalize the word I	*James*	*Letisha*		
Name on the paper	*Tommy*	*Kristen*	*Maria*	*Letisha*
Date on the paper	*Letisha*	*James*	*Kristen*	
Period at the end of the piece	*Kristen*	*Tommy*	*Maria*	*James*
Use a color word	*Tommy*	*Letisha*		
Use a question hook	*Kristen*	*James*	*Maria*	

This gives children the opportunity to get up and move purposefully and to get public recognition for their accomplishment. The concrete nature of the task enhances the editing experience.

Editing Material and Rubrics

Younger students are more enthusiastic about editing when they utilize concrete objects to aid in the exercise.

- First graders like to have small, red sticker-dots to use as Stop Signs to indicate where periods belong.
- Young editors can use a rubber stamp of a set of lips and a red ink pad to surround what came out of a speaker's mouth, the first step in dialogue punctuation.

- Finger-spacing popsicle sticks or tongue depressors, decorated at one end to look like fingernails, help emergent writers separate their consonant strings.

Young writers are not happy with commercial editing checklists. You might see an excellent checklist in a magazine or teacher's resource book, and it seems like such a good idea. You run off copies and distribute them to your students. They like new things and give it a try. But then it's nag, nag, nag, to get students to fill them out. And finally, using the check list fizzles out because it's just something else to prevent youngsters from going directly to Go and collecting $100. Like proofreaders' marks.

The only editing rubric I have seen children use consistently is a set of three boxes that kindergarten children drew themselves in the upper right-hand corner of their piece, N☐ C☐ P☐. One box was for author's name, one for a capital letter to start the whole piece, and the third for the period at the end of the entire piece. Children asked peer editors to check their papers, place a ☑ in the boxes and to put their initial under the ones they found. (You might create an ink stamp for this to make it easier for young writers.)

```
                                              N☑  C☐  P☑
                                              R.K.      R.K.

    mi cat iz on hiz bd  mi cat iz a sleap.

                                              Angela Forte
```

Other Workshop Editing Procedures

Just Do It

Teach young writers to make corrections in pencil on each other's papers. If they make an editing error, it is easily erased. This physical editing — changing a small letter to a capital letter, for example — accustoms young writers to having peer editors write on their work. If editing with corrections is practiced in the spirit of helpfulness in the primary-grade writing community, writers become used to it and will not balk at peers writing on their papers in later grades. They need to see it as the normal editing function it is.

Standard English

Use young writers' sense of language syntax as the basis of editing by ear for end punctuation. If students do not speak standard English, you will have to model it often. Pair each student with a partner who speaks standard English and encourage prewriting talking between them. These students will need more choral-reading-experience in a small group, with all the children reciting the text.

Daily Oral Language

Daily Oral Language, called DOL, is another form of editing practice. It requires children to edit two or three sentences, presented on the board or by overhead projection, that contain mistakes of grammar, capitalization, punctuation, and spelling. The sentences may also contain one or two new words for vocabulary development. Many teachers use this as their morning settling-down routine.

In *Caught'Ya! Grammar With a Giggle*, author and teacher Jane Bell Kiester[2] shows how to turn DOL into a jolly activity. Instead of using three random sentences, Kiester presents sentences in the form of an ongoing story.

There is no reason why teams of students can't create the sentences themselves. In making up the mistakes for the samples, children reinforce their own editing skills.

When you write DOL sentences on the board, be sure to demonstrate the wrapping principle. Draw the outline of a paper on the board and make it small enough that a moderate length sentence continues (wraps) on the second line. Help stamp out Single Sentence Syndrome (see Chapter 3).

Conventions as Target Skills and Editing Standards

Make grade-appropriate writing conventions some of the target skills for each marking period. Present them through minilessons, call for them in writing, ask writers to identify them in peer conferences, make them part of class editing and publishing standards. In late first, and early second grade, emphasize: capitals for the first letter in a sentence, the word *I*, and names; and a period, question mark, or exclamation mark at sentence-end.

Young writers want their work to be read, understood, and enjoyed. They will discover that to bring this about, they must follow conventions.

---

[2]*Caught'Ya! Grammar With a Giggle*, Jane Bell Kiester, Maupin House Publishing, Gainesville, FL. 1990

Editing for Spelling

Children know that there is a conventional way to spell words. Parents tend to focus on spelling as a manifestation of good writing, and children pick up on that.

Research has shown that spelling is developmental in nature: that children who use temporary spelling as they learn to write do learn to spell. The research also shows that undue emphasis on spelling while a child is *learning to write* is counterproductive. Too early an emphasis results in children writing only the words they can spell, thus severely limiting the development of their writing fluency.

Professional journals, writing-resource books, and teachers' instructional magazines abound with information about teaching spelling. Here, I am concerned only with strategies primary students can use to edit their manuscripts in preparation for presentation and publication.

I believe that classroom editing standards for primary-grade writers should include only a few spelling conventions that children can achieve independently. Typical spelling-editing standards for publishing might require the following words be spelled correctly:

Kindergarten, by mid-year
- your name
- basic color words

First grade, by mid-year-additionally
- content words, i.e., topic words you took from a class chart or book
- the primary colors and numbers one to ten

First grade, second half of year-additionally
- days of the week
- the Dolch Primary Level-One words

When children are ready to publish, tell them that they are responsible for the spelling-editing of the class standards and that you will do the rest if they like. In each succeeding grade, students assume more responsibility for the edits they can do independently, and the teacher does less.

In adulthood, writers learn to depend on peer proofreaders for a final check. Poor spellers — it's genetic isn't it? — always have a good speller check their work. Or, they use a computer spell check (which has its limitations). Most important is that writers learn the strategies that will result in a well-edited published piece.

The following models or classroom practices will help primary students edit many of the words they use.

Locating Content Words

In first grade, start one of your daily writing workshops by introducing the concept of content words.

- Show students the following paragraph with the underlines removed. Write the sentences on the easel or blackboard, or project them using a transparency. Read the paragraph chorally. Ask them, *What is this writing about? That's right, kittens. Which words are cat or kitten words?* Underline them as they find them.

    Kittens are baby cats. They purr. They have fur and whiskers. They have pads on their paws, and they have claws that they can pull back in.

- Now, tell students *These are the content words, the words that are specific to the topic, kittens.*

- Prior to the model, look through some of your writers' picture-prompted practice pieces. Find several that have content words. After you present your model of content words, ask the authors of those pieces to read them aloud. Invite children to identify the content word(s).

- After the model, follow up by having children read their own and their classmates' papers to identify their topics and the content words. Invite some of them to share pieces with the whole class and name the content words. Invite them to underline these.

- Present this model several times before asking young writers to find content words independently.

- Finally, ask writers to include this exercise when they edit to publish. Have them underline words they think are content words. They should look them up on class charts, in books and magazines they might have used, or should ask for help spelling them.

Your model

Create several models of content words in short paragraphs. Write them in the space provided. Tab the page to find it quickly.

Class Content-Word List

Whenever you teach a thematic unit or your children have a shared experience such as a field trip, assembly, or visitor, create a content-word classroom chart for writers to use as an editing resource.

First graders had written about their trip to a zoo. The prewriting and planning work had resulted in excellent pieces. The authors were going to publish these pieces in the computer lab. The teacher had collected them, fully prepared to correct the spelling before her students typed them.

She invited me to her class to demonstrate editing by ear for end punctuation. When the young writers worked in editing partnerships, many of them began asking us how to spell the words for animals they had seen. I suggested we make a list of animal words and asked the children to take the responsibility for correcting their zoo trip content words.

The children all helped construct the list and eagerly worked to correct each other's animal words. This was something they could do on their own and they were proud of it.

Great Big New Words

Children love big words. They want to use them and they want to spell them. When they ask for the spelling of new words, write them on adhesive notes and fix these to their desks for the day. Encourage them to use these when they talk about their writing and as often as they can. If they keep a word bank, have them enter these there as well.

Invite your students to make up a name for big new words: Megawords, Dinowords, Whopperwords, Tyrannosauruswords. Make a big deal of using them. Children love this kind of enthusiasm from their teachers, and they like special vocabulary and rituals reserved just for them, just for their class. That builds community.

Personal Word Banks

Word banks are collections of words a writer uses or needs that are related to his personal interests. When children ask for an uncommon word, one that is not displayed on the wall or easily located, write it for them and have them enter it in their personal word banks.

Word banks can be organized in a variety of ways:
- on cards with a hole punched in the corner, collected on a key ring
- on an 8¹/₂" by 11" oak tag or press-board sheet, covered with self-adhesive labels for the word entries, and stored in the writer's folder
- in a booklet with a page for each starting letter. (First graders should enter the primary colors with a splotch of each color beside it's name, the days of the week, and the numbers from one to ten.)

Use Spelling Pictionaries

Spelling pictionaries are available for all ages of writers. Younger writers love pictionaries in which words are illustrated and collected by category. They are less intimidating for young writers than a regular dictionary. They often contain spaces for students to create their own banks of high-frequency and content words.

Class Word Banks

Use the lower half of your classroom walls, sides of filing cabinets, desks, and cupboards to post laminated word-cards. The cards should be attached with Velcro, tacky clay, or magnets, or fixed with clothespins to wires strung beneath blackboards or bulletin boards so young writers can take them back to their desks or tables to use as models. In kindergarten and first grade, a small picture of the word on the card helps children locate them.

For the kindergarten emergent writer, the wall word banks are more useful than a personal spelling dictionary. Word models can be found quickly, and the banks promote students helping one another. A class-wall word bank helps youngsters develop independence for writing common words. Add to that the concrete aspect of the activity as well as the chance to get up and move about legitimately, and the unquestionable value of the practice is clear.

Collect Environmental Print: Labels and Signs

Many emergent writers can recognize words in **context** that they might not recognize in print text. *That says STOP*, they say when they are in the car at a stop sign. *That says Cheerios®*, they say at the breakfast table. Have children collect food labels, cereal packages, and magazine pictures of food words they can read.

They should cut and paste the words they can read on a large class chart. Write the word to the right of the drawing and again on cards to separate them from their context. Invite children to write about the foods they eat.

Build Class Charts

A useful verb chart for emergent writers is a set of drawings in which stick figures are doing something. Each figure is labeled with the verb demonstrated.

Build this chart after a minilesson in your daily writing workshop. Tell students that readers like action in writing. Model action in a picture or in writing at the easel. Or, use a large photograph or art print. Tell what is happening. Write: *T b iz s...ming. The boy is s...ming. The boy is swimming.* Underline '<u>ing</u>.'

On the chart, make a stick figure of a swimmer and label it, *swimming.* Have children say the word slowly, hearing the starting consonant, *s,* and the *ming* at the end.

For ESOL students or children who are slow to develop sound-to-symbol relationships, write the sentence: *The boy is _____ing.* Have them cut out a picture of a person doing something. Show them how to draw a stick figure over the figure in the picture. Have them tell what the person is doing. Next, have them copy the sentence format, above, and fill in the blank with at least the starting consonant. Have them find the word on the chart. If their picture is not shown, add it to the chart and put their initials after it; their contribution to a class chart is documented.

Picture-prompted writing lessons that focus on *What's happening?* need to be repeated often. Young writers need verbs to get beyond static pictures and static writing. *This is my dog. It is a house. There is a tree. There is a car.* Is is not where it's at. We want action.

Things That Can Go Wrong When Teaching Conventions and Editing

The Literal End

A first-grade teacher followed the principle of writers editing each other's work. But to keep order and quiet, she asked her children to edit for periods visually. When many of the children put periods at the end of every line, she considered independent editing a failure. Their papers looked like this:

> I ride my bike to the park and my mom.
> took me and my brother to the park I fell.
> off my bike. I got hurt

This is a good example of how young children tend to interpret information literally and concretely; in this case, the instruction to put a period at the end of each sentence. They think of *the end* as a physical location and view the word string on each line as a sentence. They thus placed periods on the right hand side of the paper where each string ended. The key factor was that these young writers did not yet understand the abstract notion of a sentence.

The teacher said to me, *This doesn't work. It's a case of the blind leading the blind.* She was prepared to drop class-editing until she had taught lessons about subjects and predicates. I convinced her to work on **choral reading** and to model **editing by ear** for periods. I modeled those aural procedures for her class. She pursued them and had enough success to continue with independent editing.

All One Long Sentence

Many young writers write everything they know in one long sentence. Their pieces might look like this.

> *I have a dog and he is brown and white and he hides under my bed and he hides his toys and I love my dog.*

First graders would have a hard time dealing with a peer's piece such as this one when they tried to clap or cluck the periods. Therefore, along with teaching editing for end punctuation, you will need to show young writers that the repetitive *and* is hard on the reader because there is no place to catch a breath. Show them how to break a long message into smaller bites.

Focusing on Conventions Before Content

The National Council of Teachers' research in writing-education practices during the last ten years substantiates the thesis that studing grammar is not an effective way to teach writing." Ira Clark, English Department, University of Florida (April 1996), in support of stringent writing entrance essays, said, "Freshmen come in with horrendous fundamental problems — like punctuation and spelling. This can be fairly easily corrected. The students that really bother you are those who can't organize, who don't elaborate, who can't construct arguments that are supported by sub-arguments and backed up by data."

We need to keep our writing education priorities in mind. Writing is thinking and communicating our ideas. If we put too great and early an emphasis on conventions as we teach children to write, we end up with writers whose papers may be correct and neat, but are devoid of information, feeling, conviction, and organized thoughts and ideas.

Chapter 10
Publishing

Young writers love to publish. Whether they read their pieces in Author's Chair, hang their work on the family's refrigerator, or publish a small hand-made book, they are proud of the accomplishment. Publishing is a natural part of the writing process.

Invite your young writers to publish early in the school year. In kindergarten and first grade, class collections of one-page-per-writer are easy to assemble. Very young writers do not copy over, but cut out their pictures and writing and paste them on the more substantial pages of a class book or display. Display and read early published work in the classroom. Later, after editing standards have been established and editing procedures have been modeled, published work can go out to the world.

Hand-publishing Activities

Publishing is project work and should be done during project time, not during the writing workshop. Primary teachers often enlist the help of older students or volunteers during a publishing project. It can be done during the course of a week or two, working with groups of children.

How-to-Hand-Publish-Young-Writers'-Work articles abound in teachers professional magazines. Your art teacher or colleagues probably know some techniques as well. Hand-published books include pop-up books, triaramas, step books, hard-cover books, slit books, flip books, and more.

Class Collections and Class Books

Class collections are the easiest way to publish young writers' work. Each student's contribution is small, no more than a page. The text is written in pencil, and the books stay in the classroom. During the year, young writers reading the class collection may suggest edits to an author. The author can change the text.

Display these books and encourage writers to read their contribution to peers. If a writer has used a target skill under study, read her work, along with professional examples from children's literature, when you model that skill. Show the children that you value their writing and that model-worthy work is within their reach.

Cut and Paste Publishing

Cut pictures and sentences from emergent writers' work to build a class book. Computer generated text also can be cut and pasted into a class book with the young writer's original drawing.

All Kinds of Books

- **ABC books:** *A is for...* with pictures. Emergent writers can draw or cut and paste pictures of objects that start with the letters of the alphabet. They can copy the phrase *A is for..., B is for...*, etc. Some can write the name of the object, as well. Or, at least the starting consonant. Write the name of the object for them if they ask.

- **Repetition books** are based on simple repetitive phrases such as *I love cats, I love Mom, I love school. Or, Apples are red. Fire engines are red. Stop signs are red.* Emergent writers in the inventorying stage love to make these.
- **Attribute books** present an inventory of objects that share an attribute. An example is Red — *Red is for stop. Red is for apple. Red is for flag stripes.*
- **All-About books** present lists of facts about a topic — usually one fact-sentence per page — and are illustrated with drawings or pasted pictures. For example: *Plants are green. We can eat some plants. Plants make the world beautiful. We make things out of plants.* These may be class collections or individual books written after a theme study.
- **Shape books** are a kind of All-About book with the pages and cover taking the shape of the subject. For example, a cloud book, a whale book, a dinosaur book.
- **Rhyming and Word-Families books** are ideal for emergent writers who inventory or copy letters.

My Writing

Publish children's work by simply clipping their papers together and binding them in folded colored art paper or wrapping paper. Title it: *My Writing*. Keep this in school. Writers can continue editing their work throughout the marking period.

Traveling Class Book

Start a first- or second-grade class book and send it to a succession of schools across the country. Enclose a cover letter describing the project, asking schools to add a specific amount to the manuscript and to send it on. Ask them to do this within a prescribed and reasonable amount of time. Ask the class that finishes it, to return it to your class. Read the returned book to your class and ask young writers to comment on the content and style.

The United States Post Office will deliver your book to:
A First-Grade Class c/o Teacher
Any Elementary School
Town/City, State, Zip code. (Specify the name of the town, state, and zip code)

The class books should be about topics that are likely to be common to all school children across the country. Some titles might include:
Our School
Our Favorite Books
Our Favorite Class Game
Our Favorite Songs
Our Best Field Trip

Best-work Board

Hang a different set of children's self-selected best work every two weeks. Invite classmates to read the board and to add compliment stickers for things they think are well done.

*　*　*

Although publishing may seem like the end of the writing process, in another sense it is the starting point. *Publishing is a great writing motivator.* Hand-published books and ready-to-use blank books, invite children to write.

What's Next

What's next is all the good stuff about writing that most of us never learned in school. It is what I call writing content. It's the techniques and characteristics of the major genres: expository and narrative writing. It's composing and literary skills, and writing conventions. Add the teaching of this content to the writing process in a daily writing workshop and you have the sure-fire formula for a successful and effective writing program.

Section Three: Writing Content in the Primary Grades

Chapter 11
A Curriculum of Target Skills

If children write often, they will gain mechanical fluency — and this is a significant primary-grade goal. But writing every day does not guarantee that children will acquire *real writing skills* (organizing, composing, elaborating, revising). Nor does taking part in a daily writing workshop based solely on the use of the writing process ensure progress and achievement. For students to achieve composing fluency, they must do more than use pencils daily. They must learn and practice the content — the body of knowledge — of writing.

That body of knowledge consists of
- the characteristics of the expository and narrative genres — for example, ending a personal narrative with how you feel about the topic or event.
- composing and literary skills — for example, using comparisons or onomatopoeia.
- writing conventions of punctuation, capitalization, and spelling — for example, starting a sentence with a capital letter.

I call these skills, **Target Skills**. They are the skills you will teach in daily writing workshop through modeling and direct instruction.

The lessons described in this section focus on *description, personal-informational expository* (telling what you know), and personal narrative (telling what happened, a personal experience). These genres are well-suited to the concrete developmental level and the egocentricity of primary children. When children write about themselves, they are engaged. They write with more detail. They know their topic well and have control of the facts. They can focus their attention, through target skills, on writing techniques.

Literature Models from All Genres

Your writing-skill lessons should be supported with literature models. Start some of your daily writing workshops reading to your students. Read from all genres: informational articles, science Big Books, news, how-to directions, poetry, and fiction. Select literature that illustrates specific writing techniques or skills your emergent writers can imitate. Direct young writers' attention to the way authors have used the techniques. Writing is a craft, and imitation is one of the best ways to learn it.

Some of the writing information and techniques that primary-grade writers can learn from this practice includes:

- the difference between expository writing (information and explanation) and narrative (story, what happened)
- telling what is happening, while looking at photos, pictures, or their own drawings
- how authors start their information pieces with a *hook* — a question, an exclamation, a noise word, etc.
- how writers like to put two words with the same sound next to each other (alliteration), *A cat caught a cute little mouse*
- how to make noise words (onomatopoeia)
- how writers use A-B-C order in some of their information books

- how writers clump related information together
- how writers of directions use words such as *Next, After that*, and *Finally* (sequence transitions)
- how writers tell their feelings about an event
- how to identify story characters, setting, and plot (what the main character wants and how he gets it)
- how writers have animals talking in a story (anthropomorphism)
- how writers use time-orienters such as *Later, After that, While, The next day.*

When children listen as writers, to both expository and narrative literature, they discover the magic link between reading and writing. When you model the writing techniques found in all genres of literature, young writers make the exciting discovery that they can do some of the same things *real authors do.*

Planning What to Teach

If your school has a coordinated writing program, an excellent approach to planning your curriculum of lessons is to do it with colleagues at your grade level. If, however, you are pioneering a daily writing workshop, present and explain your plan to your administrator. Find other teachers in your school and district who conduct daily writing workshop and ask for their help.

First: Link State or County Curriculum Requirements to Writing-Content Target Skills

With or without grade-level colleagues, make a list of the skills you are required to teach by state or county mandate. Try to find as many language arts skills as possible that can be bundled — skills that can be taught in an integrated manner in your daily writing workshop. For example, many primary-grade curricula list oral- and aural-skill benchmarks: *Student will be able to relate an event, or repeat a set of directions of no more that two steps.* These skills will be addressed naturally in daily writing workshop when young writers pre-write and share their writing. You can link language arts benchmark skills, such as *Student will be able to write complete sentences, use end punctuation, and capitalize the first word of a sentence,* to editing by ear, copying dictation, and sentence-strip reading that your young writers will do in writing workshop.

Next: Plan Writing-Workshop Increments

With a manageable list of required skills, plan your lessons in appropriate and reasonable increments; two- to four-week blocks are appropriate in the primary grades. Select several target skills for each block: a genre technique, a writing-process procedure, a literary skill, and one convention skill. Create models to demonstrate these target skills. Use the models to demonstrate printed-text principles as well, killing two birds with one stone.

For example, in a first-grade class the target skills for a two-week block might be: telling what is happening in a drawing/writing piece; using number words in picture-prompted descriptive writing; learning how to have a knee-to-knee peer conference to compliment a partner's use of the target skill; and using small letters consistently.

In daily writing workshop you will model these target skills as often as possible. You will praise children's attempts and accomplishment in Author's Chair and roving conferences. You will be on the lookout for writers who are trying to use new skills and will support them with additional individual or group lessons. You will record evidence of the skills as they appear in children's practice writing. Evaluate your emergent writers' attempts and accomplishments, not their failures.

Keep track of the stages your emergent writers are exhibiting in their writing, and plan the next printed-text concept they need to see modeled. Different writers will be at different levels, and they progress at different rates.

Grade-appropriate Target Skills

Here is a list of target skills arranged by grade. The grade reference is flexible. Be sure to examine the skills listed for the grades immediately below and/or above your grade. Typically you will have a wide range of writers in every primary grade, and their progress should be continuous. Note also that a number of skills appear throughout the primary grades, and, in fact, many of these will continue to do so in post-primary grades. What changes from grade to grade is the number and sophistication of the specific writing techniques to be taught and applied in a widening array of narrative and expository forms.

Add to this list other target skills that you teach successfully.

K	1	2	Target Skills
			Print Principles
✔	✔	✔	use finger spaces
✔	✔	✔	write from left to right
✔	✔	✔	wrap text: back to left margin and on the next line
	✔	✔	use lower case letters with increasing consistency
	✔	✔	use new page; start at the top left
			Writing Workshop/Writing Process
✔	✔	✔	pick a topic
✔	✔	✔	tell your partner what you know about your drawing/writing
✔	✔	✔	tell your partner what you see in your drawing/writing
✔	✔	✔	tell what your writing will say
✔	✔	✔	make a list (photo, pictures, letters, or words)
	✔	✔	clump information that goes together
✔	✔	✔	share your writing
✔	✔	✔	tell what your peer partner wrote
✔	✔	✔	tell your partner what your target skill is
✔	✔	✔	give a thumbs-up or compliment when you hear another writer use a target skill
✔	✔	✔	revise by adding another element or label, more color to your picture
✔	✔	✔	revise by adding another letter or word to your writing
	✔	✔	revise by adding more text at the bottom of the page
	✔	✔	revise by using a caret (^) to add a word or phrase
		✔	revise by replacing *And then* with time orienters
			Genre and Composing Skills
✔	✔	✔	use a color word, a number word, a size word
✔	✔	✔	use size, shape, age, made-from words
✔	✔	✔	use a where phrase
✔	✔	✔	use a when phrase
✔	✔	✔	use names for people and pets
	✔	✔	use specificity: Cheerios, not cereal
✔	✔	✔	ask a question
	✔	✔	use a question, exclamation, onomatopoeia for a hook
✔	✔	✔	give an opinion: I think, I know
		✔	use supporting details: prove it, who else says so, a number, a comparison
	✔	✔	end a piece by telling how you feel about the topic
✔	✔	✔	tell/write what is happening
✔	✔	✔	tell/write what happened
		✔	tell who, what, when, where at the start of a narrative

(continued on next page)

K	1	2	**Target Skills**
			Genre and Composing Skills continued
	✔	✔	write a caption for a picture
✔	✔	✔	use labeled diagrams to explain
	✔	✔	construct simple tables to organize information
			Literary Skills
✔	✔	✔	make a comparison: bigger, best, as big as a horse
✔	✔	✔	use a noise word (onomatopoeia)
	✔	✔	use rhyming words
	✔		use alliteration
		✔	use hyperbole
			Conventions
✔	✔	✔	your name on the paper
✔	✔	✔	the date on your paper (use a date stamp)
✔	✔	✔	a period at the end of all your writing
✔	✔	✔	edit by ear for a period at the end of a sentence
	✔	✔	use a capital letter to start your writing
✔	✔	✔	use a capital letter for I
	✔	✔	edit to correct your spelling of color words and the numbers one to ten
	✔	✔	capitalize first letter of names
		✔	edit to spell content and common sight words correctly

Young writers try out the genre, composing, and literary skills, on a limited basis and often orally, during your lessons at the start of daily writing workshop. They then try to apply them in their writing. They will not use them correctly or gracefully to start. Many will not use them at all. Praise both attempts and successes.

Some young writers who do not use a skill in their writing will try to use the technique following a peer conference. When their partners say, *You don't have a color word*, or, *You didn't use a question for a hook*, they add the missing element. Every writer has his own way of using his knowledge during the writing process.

Presenting a Writing-skill Lesson

Here is the sequence in which to present a writing-skill lesson. The presentation occurs during the course of several days or weeks and is reiterated throughout the school year. As you will see, the sequence includes demonstration, approximation (oral and written), practice, application, response, and finally, self-evaluation.

- Introduce the skill or technique in a starting component of daily writing workshop. Use modeled writing, discussion, pictures, or note the skill's use in one of your young writers' pieces. (See full description of teaching the target skill on page 80.)
- Provide additional examples from literature.
- Explain the technique.
- Have students try it out orally first
- Demonstrate the technique in shared writing.
- Make the technique the target skill for the week.
- Have writers try it out in their independent writing.
- Have writers share their attempts to apply the skill in their writing.

After a lesson, young writers should

- hear or see the target skill, the technique, modeled again
- help build a class chart about that skill (when appropriate)
- try to use the skill in their independent writing
- listen or watch in peer conferences for their classmates' use of the skill
- evaluate their own writing for the use of the skill

You and your young writers do not have to do every step every time. Do what is appropriate and necessary.

Whole-class Lessons

The ideal time for a **whole-class lesson** about a writing skill is when one-third to a half of your students need the technique. Your diagnosis for need will come from reading or listening to their manuscripts. Your conferencing activities during the writing component of daily writing workshop will help you make that diagnosis.

Whole-class lessons are a preview for some of the children and a review for others. Conduct them at the easel or board where you can model the skill in your writing. Conduct short lessons in Author's Chair when a child's work exhibits a good example of the skill.

When you present a minilesson the first time, young writers will not necessarily apply the skill to their writing immediately. Rather, they will copy the model, experiment with the idea, see and hear it used by peers who were ready for the concept, or they may even ignore it.

> *Marilyn Cafaro presented a ten-minute minilesson about using onomatopoeia for a hook to her first/second grade class. Her students were writing personal narratives or personal informational pieces in their journals. (The first graders were already using questions and exclamations for their hooks.) Marilyn read an entry from one of the students' journals and said, "Listen to how Mark used noises to start his piece. 'Crash, smash. I broke my glass at supper.'"*
>
> *She wrote a few noise words on the easel to get them started. Then all the children contributed to the list. Next, Marilyn invited them to use noise words from the chart or to make up their own when they wrote in their journals.*
>
> *After talking to their partners about the writing they were planning for that day and how sounds might be part of that, the children began writing. Here is how the writing component of the workshop went:*
>
> - *Some first-graders used onomatopoeia in the first sentence of their journal entries.* Pop. Pop. We made popcorn; Splash. Splash. It rained last night.
>
> - *Two girls told me they already knew what they were going to write and there were no sounds in what happened. They asked if they had to use onomatopoeia as a hook. Of course not.*
>
> - *Some young writers (both first- and second-graders) copied all the sound words they liked from the easel and made the sounds as they wrote. Then, they made up more and drew the action that went with each sound. They never did get to the message part of their journal entries.* These writers were satisfying their inventorying urge. Application would come later.

Do not be concerned that only four or five writers grasp the presented idea. The lesson introduces the idea to the writing community. It will spread. When writers see others using the idea successfully, they will follow. Children learn quite effectively from each other.

Pat Veltz, a kindergarten teacher, told me that one day during Author's Chair a classmate said to a writer, "I can tell you are running in your picture because your legs are bent." The next day a flock of writers had bent-legged characters in their picture writing.

Group lessons

Ideally, a **group lesson** should be aimed specifically at the writers who can use the writing technique because they have been trying it on their own. Young writers who notice things in their sibling's or in adult writing often try to copy them. When they do, they are ready for the guidance of a group lesson. Group lessons are also used to help writers who are having trouble applying a target skill to their writing.

Group lessons are usually short, no more than ten to twenty minutes. The best place to give them is in a central location where any writer who wants to can eavesdrop for preview or review.

Repeating lessons

Be prepared to **repeat a lesson several times**: for the class, for a new group, or for an original group's review after a vacation.

Teaching the Target-skill Concept

The Picture-prompted Model

A picture-prompted writing model is a handy way to introduce the concept of target skills in all grades. Picture-prompted writing utilizes a photograph, magazine picture, personal snapshot, art print, or such, to stimulate ideas. The picture is a concrete aid; children can hold it, cut and paste it, feel it, talk about it. Through the use of this model, children come to understand the range or variety of techniques involved in writing. It is also an excellent vehicle for demonstrating the writing process and the associated procedures children use in daily writing workshop.

Our Visual Sense

Picture-prompted writing is a useful teaching tool because it takes advantage of children's natural and keen visual-learning mode. Human beings are a visual species. If I were teaching puppies, I would base my instruction on the sense of smell, using a collection of containers filled with various scents. Humans, however, learn mostly through their visual sense. In this age of TV and computers, the visual-learning mode has become even more dominant. Aural learning, at which those who were raised in the days of radio became adept, has declined.

Presenting the First Picture-prompted Target-skill Model

I introduce picture-prompted writing in the second or third week of school in kindergarten, and in the first week of both first and second grade. Early-stage emergent writers can do this work orally, while those in the Soundmaker Stage and beyond are ready to do it in written form. The model, which incorporates selecting a picture, pasting, talking, listening, and writing, takes two blocks of time: one for the selection, pasting, and talking, and one for the writing.

You will need a large collection of colorful pictures cut from magazines. The collection should include pictures of children engaged in play, work, sports, eating; animals: insects, birds, reptiles, mammals, fish; rural and urban scenes, and so on. Ask people to collect them for you. National Geographic magazines are a wonderful source of color photos. Collect them from garage sales or used-book stores.

Modeling picture selection and gluing the picture on greenbar, unlined paper, or in a journal

Gather your class to the meeting place. Spread an assortment of trimmed magazine pictures in front of you. Tell the children you are going to select a picture to talk and write about. Think aloud as you make your selection. *Maybe I will write about this picture. That dog looks just like my dog: same color, same floppy ears.* Or, *I could do this one: I love llamas. I even petted one once.* Or, *This picture makes me feel happy. It reminds me of my brother and how we used to go fishing together.*

Show children how you paste your picture on paper. Talk as you model: *I think I will use this paper. I think I will paste the picture in the upper corner of my paper.* Demonstrate the use of glue sticks, liquid glue dispenser, or paste. Show children how you glue just along the edges.

Place groups of 5-10 pictures on tables around the room and invite the children to browse, just as if they were in a library looking for a book. Invite each of them to select a picture. Suggest that they look **for a picture they really like, a picture about something they know, or something they can do, or of a place where they have been** — a topic that relates to their personal background and experience.

Provide paper and glue. Rove around and remind them how to use the glue sparingly. Invite children to talk about their pictures with their writing partners as they make their selection and as they glue it.

What do two young writers do when they want the same picture? Share it. Show them how to paste the picture on a very large sheet of unlined paper. Divide the text area in two for them. They will each write on one half of the paper.

Model talking about the picture to introduce the target skill

When everyone has a picture pasted on paper, call the children to the meeting place. Have them leave their pictures at their desks. Ask a child who you know is articulate to bring his or her picture to the group to be your partner. Tell the children that you and your partner are going to model a conference about the pictures.

> **Teacher:** (Place a picture of an archery target with a bull's-eye and arrow drawn in it, and labeled **TARGET**, on the easel.) *Writers try very hard to help you, their reader, see what they see. They make sure they tell what the people or animals are doing, what is happening, what colors, numbers, shapes, and sizes you would want to know about. Today I would like you to think really hard about what is happening in your picture when you tell your partner about it. That will be what you aim for when you talk and write about the picture. That will be your TARGET. Point to the target picture. Watch Jennifer and me as we try to hit the TARGET.*

> Sit across from Jennifer, knee-to-knee, and begin:

> **Teacher:** *The target is to tell what is happening in the picture. I will try to do that. Jennifer, I picked this picture because I love dogs. I have one just like this one. This dog is scrunched down behind the mailbox. I think he is waiting to pounce at the mailman. The dog is tan, like the color of a football. (Pause.) Did I hit the target? What did you hear me say was happening?*

> **Jennifer**: *I heard you say the dog was waiting to pounce on the mailman.*

> **Another student**: *And you said he was all scrunched down.*

> **Teacher**: *Good job hearing if I hit the target. Now it is Jennifer's turn.*

> **Jennifer**: *My picture is a little girl pushing her sister in a swing. Did I hit the target?*

> **Teacher**: *Yes, you did. And, you can tell anything else you like about your picture.*

Jennifer: *She looks like she likes it.*

Teacher: *How did you know that?*

Jennifer: *She is smiling.*

Teacher: *Thank you for conferencing with me. Boys and girls, you are all going to conference with your partners now. Will you try to hit the target, telling what is happening? Remember, you can say anything about your picture, but try to tell your partner what is happening — aim for the target.*

Write: *What is happening?* on the blackboard. Draw a large archery target and write: *What is happening?* in the bull's eye. Add an arrow to the bull's eye.

Begin the knee-to-knee pre-writing conferences. You may gather some young writers to work with you in a group. Encourage children to tell anything about their pictures. Invite the members of the group to give a silent thumbs-up signal when they think they hear the teller hit the target — i.e., they hear *what is happening* in the picture. Model your picture description again, using a different verb phrase than you did in your first model.

Sharing

When the children have finished conferencing (usually five minutes is sufficient), use the sharing technique of asking young writers to compliment their partners. (This technique is described in Chapter 4.) *Who heard their partners hit the target? Please tell us your partners' names and what they said was happening?* Listen to several children's examples.

Young writers will have to pay close attention as their partners talk. This fosters listening skills. Young writers will be broadcasting examples of their partners' good ideas. This contributes to the pool of writing knowledge. Peers will be giving compliments for achievement. This builds respect and a sense of community.

Model writing about the picture on the next day

Gather your children to the easel where you have placed your picture and paper. Write a big TS in the upper right-hand corner. Say: *This stands for target skill. Who remembers yesterday's target? Yes, it was: What is happening?* Write an H under the TS (TS/H). *H stands for happening.*

Under your picture, write a sentence that tells what is happening. *The girl is fishing.* Add more information for your advanced emergent writers in kindergarten and first grade. *The girl is fishing. She has a big bucket. I think she will put the fish in it.* (This is another opportunity to model left-to-right directionality and the wrapping principle of printed text. But, do not talk about that; the focus of this model is hitting the *what's happening* target.) Read the text back as you write. End with a conspicuous period. Make a clucking sound as you write the period (reinforcing your edit by ear lessons). Add your name to the page. Have children read it with you and ask them if you hit the target.

Start the writing component of your workshop, telling young writers to write anything they want about their pictures, but to try to hit the target. *Remember what you told your*

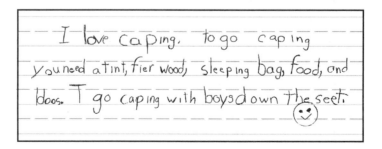

partner about the picture yesterday. Some children will ask if they can have a knee-to-knee conference to talk about the picture again. Good idea. Some children will ask if they should put TS and an H in the corner of the paper. Those who ask should do it. Let other writers see them do it. Many will copy the idea.

Close the writing workshop with an Author's Chair and/or pairs sharing before they put their writing away.

Your model:

Paste a picture here. Write what you would say about the picture as a model for students. Tab this page of the book to find this model quickly when you need it.

Model Picture-prompted Writing Again

As with all models, repeat this one from time to time, focusing on a different target skill each time. Start with a simple one, and move to a more sophisticated skill. For instance, if you start with using a color word, the next time, make the target using a comparison about the color.

Always do the exercise both orally and in writing. Here is a skill sequence you might use during the course of several months:

- Tell <u>who or what</u> is in the picture. *A little girl is talking to a friend.*
- Tell about the <u>place</u> in the picture. *This is at McDonalds.*
- Describe the <u>colors </u>in the picture. *The bird is red.*
- Use a <u>number</u> word. *I see two bears.*
- Use a <u>size</u> word. *The boy is bigger than the truck.*
- Make a <u>comparison.</u> *The bird is bigger than the egg. The girl is taller than the dog.*
- Tell what you <u>think</u>. *I think the wolf would make a good pet.*
- Use a question <u>hook</u>. *What is this bear doing?*
- Start with a capital letter.
- Use periods.

Use the picture-prompted writing model for practicing all kinds of target skills. Some teachers introduce the target skill on Monday and establish it as the target the children will use during the week in a writing center. First- and second-graders usually remember target skills from previous weeks and carry them forward.

Do not require young writers to use a magazine picture for their independent, ongoing writing. (They may do so if they like.) You will find that a few young writers have strong visions in their mind about which they choose to write, and they will not be interested in using pictures. Offer it only as an invitation. Writers must always have choices.

Other Uses For Picture-Prompted Writing

- Oral skill development: use the model for an oral exercise only. Have children look at their pictures for three minutes, then tell all about the pictures. Have them point to things they know. Have each of them listen to their partner tell about the same picture. This is a particularly useful exercise with ESOL students.

- Picture-prompted writing works well with emergent writers who are stuck in the random letter-stringing stage (Stage Three, Letter Copier). Partner them with a writer who knows the sound-letter connection. Have the partner help the child label the pictures with starting consonants, marking directly on the pictures with felt-tipped pens.

- Help children in the inventorying stage make a list of everything they see in their pictures. Put the model on the board.
    - I see a _____
    - I see a _____
    - I see a _____

- Use picture-prompted writing for descriptive writing lessons. Have young writers focus on an attribute (size, shape, color, number, position, etc. See Chapter 12). The attributes become the target skills for the picture reaction.

The bull is brown and her eyes are red.

- Use children's picture-prompted writing for modeling and practicing peer conferences, revision, and editing.

- Display picture-prompted writing on a bulletin board or by publishing it in a class or individual student collection.

- Collect a series of picture-prompted writing pieces, created during the year, for a child's portfolio to demonstrate writing progress.

- Pictures can be selected for their relation to science, social studies, art, and math to encourage associated vocabulary use. For example, to focus on math, show children how to select a picture that has multiple objects, shapes, or symmetry. Model math talking: *I see three dogs and two cats. Or, Four kids are playing kickball, and three are just standing. That makes seven kids.*

During a thematic unit, Marilyn Cafaro's first- and second-graders select pictures from Junior National Geographic, National Geographic, Ranger Rick, and other science and geography magazines. The young writers build collections of picture-prompted writing. Sometimes they prepare two to four sheets in advance.

Joshua

This is a meerkat. It has brown fur and a long tail. She is sitting in the sun looking around.

They ask her to read the captions of the pictures before they cut them from the magazines, then they use words from the captions when they write. They watch science and geography programs on TV related to the topic and report back to the class. They write words from their listening vocabulary, which is by far children's largest vocabulary in the primary grades. Speaking, writing, and reading vocabularies follow.

Precursors to Comprehensive Assessment Tests

In comprehensive assessment tests, students must write opinions, or thesis statements, after reading a selection of text that often includes a graphic (table, map, diagram, etc.). They must write about the evidence or details that support their thesis.

We can contribute to students' success in this kind of test using precursor writing activities in the primary grades. This does not mean that we will ask them to do what fourth graders are required to do on the test. (It is folly to think that we can prepare students for such exercises by simply starting at an earlier age, thinking that if they practice for a few years they will really be good at it by fourth grade. We must use grade-appropriate activities that lead to success at a later grade. We must remember to apply our knowledge of how children's brains work, i.e., our Piaget notes from Education Psychology.)

A precursor activity for successfully interpreting text is asking primary students to interpret pictures, giving an opinion and finding evidence in the picture to support their statement. A typical target skill for picture-prompted writing in kindergarten and first grade is: I think... In late-first grade and second grade, add to that target: I think.... because.... (What evidence in the picture makes you think that?)

By second grade students can write book reports in which they state an opinion about the character, setting, or plot, (brainstorm a few for them to use from a story everyone read before asking them to formulate their own). They will then cite pages and text where they found evidence to support that opinion. See page 110, Literature Response., for an example of this kind of book report about The Tale of Johnny Town Mouse.

Chapter 12
Description

Description is a good place to start a writing instruction program. Young children are naturally observant. We can use descriptive writing to make use of their natural curiosity and observational prowess. We can encourage these traits and help them build a rich vocabulary of descriptive language. Description is fundamental to all writing and supports both the expository genre, which is the natural inclination of emergent writers, and the narrative genre.

Picture-prompted writing (see Chapter 11) is a good tool to use in building that language of description. Use the following list of descriptive attributes as a source of appropriate, specific target skills when young writers respond to both pictures and their own drawings.

Descriptive Attributes

- **color**: *specific* — red, green; *comparative* — reddish, brown like a tree trunk, ...
- **size**: *specific* — three feet high; *comparative* — larger, as big as, ...
- **number**: *specific* — six, ten; *nonspecific* — many, some, several; *comparative* — more than, fewer, ...
- **shape**: *specific* — round, oval, square, triangular; *comparative* — like a box, ...
- **age**: *specific* — five-years old; *nonspecific* — old, new; *comparative* — older than my grandmother, ...
- **texture**: *specific* — smooth, rough, bumpy, lumpy, soft, fuzzy, slippery; *comparative* — stickier, bumpier, ...
- **movement or action**: *specific* — running, hopping, gliding, sliding, flapping, jumping; *comparative* — faster, slower, ...
- **location (where is it?)**: *specific* — on, over, under, in front of, next to; *comparative* — higher, lower, nearer, ...
- **composition (made from)**: *specific* — wooden, metal, plastic, cloth, glass, concrete, cardboard, paper; *comparative* — hard as a rock, smooth as glass.
- **smell**: *specific* — burnt, sweet; *comparative* — smoky, like raspberries, ...
- **taste**: *specific* — sweet, bitter, tangy, salty; *comparative* — like orange juice, sweeter than, ...
- **habitat**: for living things — underground, inside a tree, in a den, on a pond, ...
- **direction**: left, right, up, down, backward, sideways, forward, north of, ...
- **temperature**: *specific* — a hundred degrees, three below zero; *comparative* — hotter than, coldest, ...
- **weight**: *specific* — ten pounds; *comparative* — as heavy as, the lightest, ...
- **special features**: writing, stripes, polka dot, knobs, buttons, ...

Characteristics of Descriptive Writing

In descriptive writing, the writer selects, then describes, elements of a scene that have meaning to him. An interior decorator and a psychologist who visited your classroom would describe it quite differently.

The most important and interesting element to describe in writing is people (or animals) doing something. Readers want to read about living things, not inanimate objects.

They want to read about active, not static, scenes. They want to know what the writer thinks. They want to be involved, engaged. Good descriptive writing should satisfy them.

Model the following descriptive elements and techniques in the starting components of daily writing workshop. Have children try them orally. Make them the targets children can aim for in their writing.

- **people and objects seen**: who, what, number, where they are, age, condition, size, shapes, features, all the attributes listed above
- **what is happening**: people, animal, and object movements, weather conditions
- **sounds heard**: type, where it comes from, how loud it is
- **what it feels like**: textures, mood, atmosphere
- **smells**: types, where it comes from, how strong it is
- **what you are reminded of**: other places, other people, other events
- **comparison**: in its various forms — *er* and *est* words, *as* _____ *as, just like, so* _____ *that*

Observation and Description

Observation and description are fundamental to science as well as to writing. The following lessons are important science activities and language arts experiences. In the primary grades, most state and county science curricula include *observation and description* benchmarks. Children are natural scientists at this age; they are discovering things about their environment, their natural surroundings. Provide time for your students to observe and make discoveries; encourage them to talk about them.

I Spy

Before you begin to use descriptive attributes as target skills, play I SPY with your class. Model as many different attributes as you can. *I spy something red. I spy a circle. I spy something round. I spy something made of wood. I spy something furry.* Children try to guess what the person who is IT has spied. Give children a chance to be IT: to say: *I Spy...*

Play I Spy on the playground as well. Play it at the class easel, using a large art print.

Attribute Field Trip

Take your children on a field trip through the classroom, the school halls, or the school yard to find examples of descriptive attributes. Language arts field trips are as valuable as science and social studies field trips.

Give students a clipboard and a copy of an attribute list appropriate for their ages and attention spans. You can use drawings of objects, color splotches, or numbers on the list for kindergarten children to find. Their list can be a check-off type. *Something red* (a splash of red on the data sheet), *Something round* (drawing of a circle), *Something alive* (picture of a squirrel or bird).

a) Model one or two entries about the target attribute on the class list. Write them on the board. For example, in first grade, the target might be *size by comparison*. Instead of describing something by its exact size, say or write:
   It's the size of my shoe.
   It's small enough to fit in my hand.
   It's bigger than an egg.

b) Walk writers around the area selected. Young children need to get up and move about often. You can turn some of this stretch-and-move time into *academic exercise.*

c) Gather in a central place with prearranged seating and share the entries the young writers made.

Color — *a red bulletin board, a gray and yellow book bag, a dark green leaf.*
Shape — *a leaf that looks like a hand, a round shell, a square sign.*

I. <u>Attribute Hunt</u>: Find something outside, in nature, for each attribute: Describe it in just one sentence.
Example: Size - *I found a leaf that is so <u>tiny</u> a bug might use it for an umbrella.*
Or: *The brook by the library is <u>about six feet across</u>.*

Movement: __Like a helicopter!__

Shape: __rectangle__

Age: __bridge new__

Location: __the flowers are oh the free.__

Direction: __strait__

Smell: __The flowers smell like butter.__

Made of: __They are made of nature. nature__

Number: __5 small trees are in the back.__

Attribute Show and Tell

The day before this activity, ask young writers to bring in one colorful item each. Make a set of attribute cards appropriate for the children's experience and background. Use attributes from the list found at the start of this section: *color, shape, size, number, feels like, etc.*

Conduct a Show and Tell. Children tell about their objects, using as many attributes cards as they can. Or, play it as a game, with classmates holding up an attribute card and the player making up a sentence about the object using the attribute. For example, the color card is held up and the child with the object says, *My toy car is blue.* Or, the other way around — a child saying something about the object, and the class identifying which attribute the child told about. For example, *My toy car goes fast.* The class guesses the attribute, movement.

Try this activity with photographs children select from the class picture file.

Colors

As Diane Ackerman tells us in *The Natural History of the Senses*, (NY Random House, 1990) we have a rich vocabulary of descriptive words for our visual sense compared to the limited one for smell and taste. Apart from putrid, fragrant, pungent, acrid, sour, sweet, bitter, tart, and a few others, most of the words for smell and taste depend on our making a comparison to something else: *salty, spicy, musty, it smells like licorice, it smells like burnt leaves, it tastes like carrots.*

Words for colors are virtually limitless and most of them have a name. Use the biggest box of crayons to demonstrate the variety. Show children how many color names use comparisons to natural elements, such as flowers, trees, and woods — *periwinkle blue, coral, primrose, lemon yellow, mahogany, sky blue, orchid, ash blond, etc.*

Provide color-word resources for students. Ask your art teacher for other sources in addition to the following:

- Crayola® crayons: box of 64
- paint chips: dozens of cards, each with an array of six to eight named shades of one color are available at paint and hardware stores
- carpet samples: sets of 4" by 4" pieces, in an array of named colors and shades (These are especially appealing to primary students who love to run their hands over the carpet.)
- new-car color charts from local car dealers

Textures

Create a collection of textures. Mount samples on masonite panels or heavy card stock. Paste pieces of fur, carpet, velvet, sandpaper, vinyl, Velcro, etc. on the panels. Invite students to add other samples. Make a class chart of words to describe these textures. Use children's words first, even made-up words. Add to the chart as you and children find a texture word when you read aloud to them. Place a child's initials after a contribution to the chart.

Verbs

Build a class chart on which children paste an action picture. You or they can write the verb it portrays under the picture.

Ask young writers to tell or write a description using a family photo or a picture they have selected from the classroom file. They are to base their description entirely upon *what is happening* in the picture. Before they write the description, ask them to list all the action words — verbs — that apply to the picture. Call the children's attention to a word bank of verbs illustrated with stick figures in action (see Chapter 9).

Paragraph model:

> *This is my family playing ball. My brother Tom is the one pitching. He always throws too low. We yell at him to play fair. My sister Paula is at second base, trying to steal third. She didn't make it. Tom tagged her out.*

Your model:

> Paste a class or family photo here and write a few sentences about what is happening. Use big, fat, juicy, grade-appropriate verbs: *power verbs, megaverbs, strong verbs.* Point out strong verbs when you read to your class.

Shapes

Integrate geometry and writing by using plane and three-dimensional shapes as the source of descriptive vocabulary. Once you have introduced geometric shapes to the children in math, take your writers on a short field trip to find these shapes in the natural and architectural environment. Set a limited goal of finding and describing two geometric shapes. Model talking about geometric shapes before you go outside.

> *I see a triangle. It is the slide and the ground.*
> *The red sign in front of the school is a square.*

Use a check-off sheet for kindergarten children.

When you return to class, ask the children to draw one of the shapes they saw or a shape they see in the room. Model writing about a shape that you draw on the easel. For example, draw the loops of the chain holding a swing. Write: *I saw something round. It was in the swing's chain.*

Shape or features	I see
Round ○	
Square □	
Triangle △	
Striped ≡	
Dotted ∴	
Crossed ✕	

Sounds

Compared to sights, we have a limited vocabulary for sounds. We extend it by making up words that imitate the sound: *Splash, whir, pbzzt, kerplop,* ... This is called *onomatopoeia.* Young writers love Peter Spier's onomatopoeia books, *Crash! Bang! Boom!,* and *Gobble Growl Grunt.* (See bibliography at the end of this chapter.)

We can describe sounds by their source and intensity as well as their quality. Take your class outside for a sound field trip. Seat the class in a comfortable, shady spot, and ask youngsters to identify one or two sounds. *Can you describe them? Where does it come from? Is it loud or soft? Is it pretty or is it annoying?* You should do this as an oral exercise. Later, invite the children to use sound words in their writing. When you read to your class, show them when an author uses onomatopoeia.

Publish Attribute Books

Attribute books focus on one attribute and give illustrations of it — *red is for apples, red is for fire trucks, red is for stop.* Or, they focus on one object and give all its attributes — *apples are red, apples are round, apples are yummy.*

Writers of all ages enjoy making attribute books. They can be presented as shape books, too.

Scientific Description

Observation and description and **sorting and classification** are among the most important skills a scientist needs. If we do nothing else in elementary school science but help children to become adept at these skills, we will have prepared them well for science study throughout the rest of their lives.

A. Use the picture-prompted technique described in Chapter 11. Create a file of science-theme pictures, or collect Junior and regular National Geographic magazines that contain articles about the science theme you are studying: insects, mammals, ocean life, habitats, plants, etc. Have children make a booklet of their picture-prompted writing collection about that theme. Post the content words for the theme and make their correct spelling the editing standard for the project.

B. Show children how to sort and classify objects and living things. Help them make graphic data organizers such as the following table. Help them summarize their observations using the organizers. Keep them simple.

Button	Color	Number of holes
1	red	4
2	white	2
3	white	4
4	brown	2

Other things to examine and record:
    toys: color, wheels (yes or no)
    classmates names: eye color, hair color
    books: number of pages, photos or drawings
    leaves: color, edges (like a saw or smooth)
    flowers: color, number of petals
    stuffed animals: color, tail (yes or no)

Invite students to write a simple sentence or more from their observation data such as, *The leaf is dark green. It has edges like a saw.* Or, *The blue car has four wheels.* Or, *The cat has a tail. The eyes are black and white buttons.*

Comparison

Imaginative comparisons are a wonderful way by which authors create the imagery necessary to put readers into a scene. Encourage young writers to compose a fresh and vivid comparison with such questions as, *What did it look like to you? What did it seem like to you?* Emphasize the word, *like*.

> *The cars were crawling like ants.*
> *It's sticky like pancake syrup.*

Similes, metaphors, and analogies are the names of devices used for making comparisons. A simile compares two things using the form: as _____ as _____: *The cheetah is as fast as the wind.* A metaphor compares by speaking of one thing as if it were another, meaning it has the characteristic attribute associated with the named thing. *He is an ox,* meaning he is as strong as an ox. Analogies show how two things relate to each other in the same way. *Writing is like composing music. Just because you can read music doesn't mean you can compose a symphony. Just because you can read a book doesn't mean you can write one.*

Young writers can start with making simple comparisons using *er* and *est*. *A whale is bigger than a bus.* Some children will naturally use similes (*My dog is as tall as a pony.*) When you find children who can compare in this fashion, support them with a lesson about similes. Encourage them to use these in their writing.

Writing Directions

Model the process physically — concretely. Walk your students from your room to the art room or gym. At each decision point stop and ask, *Where do I go next?* Or, *Which way do I turn now?* Write it on a clipboard as you go. Read it back to the children as you take the same walk again. This activity can be used to reinforce the concepts of left and right or up and down (stairs).

Invite partners to write directions to parts of the room from their desks or table. Take your children outside and work on oral directions to parts of the playground. Encourage children to draw simple maps or diagrams to accompany their directions. Model a series of pictures to illustrate each step in a process or each place you see as you follow directions.

A Word About Adjectives

I have deliberately avoided the use of the word *adjective* in the previous material about description. Good description depends heavily on verbs, as well as description-implicit nouns (e.g., *igloo*, instead of *house*). The best descriptive writing is kinetic — writing in which the reader visualizes characters and scenes as if they were in a film rather than a static picture. Action words, verbs, are the key to achieving this kind of vivid descriptive writing. Help young writers focus on *what's going on, what's happening, and specificity.*

When we call adjectives *describing words*, we may inadvertently lead young writers to think that they should use adjectives preferentially when they describe. In the intermediate grades they will write descriptions consisting of adjective lists, sounding something like this: *Little kids in large, red, fuzzy, wool mittens* are catching *big, round, white, cold snowballs.* Not very graceful.

Adjectives are fine if they perform a meaningful function in description. Is the adjective specific? Is it appropriate to the meaning we want to convey or is it worn out and trite? We should particularly warn older writers to avoid redundant adjectives — ones that describe an attribute already implied in the nouns they modify, such as *green grass, sandy beach, a hot fire, white snow, furry kitten.* Emergent writers will probably not understand that concept, so the best way to approach it is to avoid drumming the phrase — *adjectives are describing words* — into their heads.

For your professional reading in description, I strongly recommend:

- Ackerman, Diane. *A Natural History of the Senses.* New York: Random House, 1990.
- Hall, Susan. *Using Picture Storybooks to Teach Literary Devices.* Phoenix, AZ: Oryx Press, 1990.
- Hanson, Joan. *More Similes: roar like a lion.* Minneapolis, MN: Lerner Publications Co., 1979.
- Juster, Norton. *As: a surfeit of similes.* New York: Morrow Junior Books, 1989.
- Spier, Peter. *Crash! Bang! Boom!* Garden City, NY: Doubleday and Company, Inc., 1972.

Chapter 13
Personal Expository

Expository writing is about facts or information, feelings, explanations, directions, opinions, ideas, and argument. Expository writing is the writing we are required to do for the rest of our lives. It is the genre of literature response, of reading-comprehension questions, of academic test questions. It is the genre of the work-a-day world. Cherish and nurture this form of writing.

There is *no passage of time* in expository writing as in narrative. Expository prose is usually, but not exclusively, *written in the present tense*. It has a purpose or objective — to inform, explain, convince, amuse, etc. Writers *organize* expository prose by *clumping* related information and ideas together. In your lessons about this genre, you will point this out to emergent writers, model it, and have them try it out in a concrete fashion.

The easiest and most logical start to instruction in this genre is personal, informational expository. In short, this means writers telling what they know. (Essay is the expository form that deals with abstract concepts, ideas, opinion, and argument. Its introduction is appropriate to children entering the formal- and abstract-thinking stage — about the age of ten, according to Piaget.)

Emergent Writers' First and Natural Mode is Personal and Informational Writing

Personal, informational expository writing is based on concrete facts and feelings. Children are eager to share what they know when they write in this mode. They are emotionally connected to their topics and can write passionately about them.

> *This is my house.*
> *I love my mom. I love my grampa. I love my teacher. I love my teddy bear.*
> *I have a dog. He is brown. He has floppy ears. He licks my face.*
> *This is my rabbit. She eats carrots. And she likes me.*

Personal, informational writing presents no knowledge barriers and no motivation barriers. The child can place almost his entire attention on acquiring the writing skills that will let him tell what he knows. In addition, all the principles and techniques of good writing can be applied to the genre. It is easy to see why this is the easiest and best place to begin writing instruction. Later, as the young writers' general knowledge grows, they can write pure informational pieces about the things they have learned but have not experienced personally.

Read Informational Expository Literature to Your Students

Develop students' ear for the expository genre by reading it to them frequently. Read books about a theme, moving in a natural progression from an information book to a story. For example, you might read an article or science Big Book about eggs hatching and follow that with *Are You My Mother* (the story of a hatchling who came out of his shell while his mother was off the nest and asks everyone and everything, "Are you my mother?") by P. D. Eastman, NY: Random House, Beginner Books, 1960.

- Demonstrate that information books are enjoyable. Select them for their beautiful illustrations. Use emergent reading series that are informational and photo-illustrated. Read children's picture books that are not stories — not organized chronologically. Some examples are:

  Aliki. *My Hand*. New York: Thomas Y. Crowell, 1990.
  Arnosky, Jim. *Come Out Muskrats*. New York: Lothrop, Lee and Shepard Books, 1989.
  Browne, Anthony. *I Like Books*. New York: Alfred A. Knopf, 1988.
  Browne, Anthony. *Things I Like*. New York: Alfred A. Knopf, 1989.
  Freeman, Marcia. *Wetlands*. New York: Newbridge, 1998.
  Gibbons, Gail. *Dogs*. New York: Holiday House, 1996.
  Kenhardt, Edith. *I Want to Be a Farmer*. New York: Grosset and Dunlap, 1989.
  Paulsen, Gary. *The Tortilla Factory*. New York: Harcourt Brace and Co., 1995
  Sweeny, Joan. *Me on the Map*. New York: Crown Publishers, Inc., 1996.
  Wax, Wendy and Rowland, Dell. *10 Things I Know About Whales*. New York: Contemporary Books, Inc., 1989.

- Read science Big Books, *Ranger Rick Magazine*, *Junior National Geographic*, directions to games, advertisements, invitations, letters to be sent home, book reviews, and the About-the-Author information from the fiction books you read to your class.

When you read informational books, not only are you helping children develop an ear for expository genre, but they are also learning facts about nature, science, history, social studies, cooking, art, music, books, sports, etc. Your reading aloud does double duty.

Use Expository Writing Vocabulary

Call emergent writers' natural informational writing your *writing; your piece; your picture/ writing; your manuscript, your article*. Do not call it *your story*, as in, *Bring your story to Author's Chair; Let me hear your story; What is your story about?* — unless you know it *is* a story.

When children share their piece in Author's chair, coach them to tell their audience what kind of writing they have done. Ask them, *Are we going to learn something, or is this about what happened?*

Encourage children to respond with specific statements such as. *This is what I know about dogs; This is something for you to learn; This is what I saw at the zoo; This is what I know about manatees; This is an information piece; This is expository writing.*

Do not require that your emergent writers write *stories* as the preferred genre in writing workshop. Do not require that they write fables, fairy tales, and fiction. Fiction is a difficult genre for the best of writers. (A few children, who have a flair for fiction, and who probably have had stories read to them since infancy, will naturally attempt it.

Do support them with lessons to help them write graceful fiction. But be sure they learn the techniques associated with expository writing, as well.)

Picture Captions

Read and re-read informational Big Books. After your class is familiar with the text and photo-illustrations, have young writers listen to how the author tells about the pictures. Use emergent-level, photo-illustrated informational books to show children how to use a picture for clues to the words in the text. Invite them to write their own photo-illustrated booklets.

Teresa Morey invited me to her first-grade class to read my book, Push and Pull, a physical-science Big Book about forces (Newbridge Educational Publishing, 1997). On the following day, she re-read the book to her class, and the children demonstrated pushing and pulling. Then, Teresa asked the children to find a magazine picture that showed pushing or pulling and to write a one-sentence caption about the picture (pasted on a sheet of primary paper). Here is one of them:

You can discover if children understand a concept you are teaching by seeing what they write. If they understand the concept, they will be able to write about it, as these first graders did, imitating the author.

Using Graphics to Present Information

Encourage children to use diagrams and simple tables to present information. As the saying goes, a picture is worth a thousand words. This is particularly so when young children write to explain.

pull Austen	push
	Close the dor
pull the dro	push a wagin
Open dor	Clos the Book
tren the light off	seenk plug
open the Book	

Model the construction of maps, tables, graphs, diagrams, cross-sections, and such often in your informational writing. Share informational literature with them that contains a variety of graphic informational displays. Help the children discover what each graphic tells, and have them articulate what they learn from it.

Diagrams can be labeled drawings to show parts of things, a series of drawings to show the steps in a process, or a simple map. (Primary children's maps show location of objects but do not necessarily show them from a bird's-eye view. They combine an overhead view with side views.)

Help children construct simple graphs by pasting the objects they count on paper. This is a typical manipulative math activity. Have children write a sentence or two about the graph: *What does it show us?*

Organization: Primary Style

The youngest writers, who are not able to construct abstract, graphic writing planners such as webs and outlines, and who may not organize their writing logically, can, nonetheless, learn some techniques that are precursors to organized writing. Making comparisons and sorting are two of these.

Comparison

To compare means to show both similarities and differences. (To contrast means to show only differences. It is therefore redundant to tell students to *compare and contrast.*)

The following two lesson models use concrete objects to enhance the learning experience. Through the use of Flip Books and Venn Diagrams, children can begin to understand how to compare real objects. In Sorting and Clumping, and Precursor to Paragraphing on page 101, you will see how they can move from the comparison of real things to the comparison of written information.

Flip books

Conduct this lesson about comparison well after you have introduced descriptive attributes through picture-prompted writing. Take several days to present the three steps of the lesson. Use writing workshop or science time.

You will need a collection of 12-15 object pairs that have some similarities and differences. For example: pairs of stuffed animals, toy cars, shoes, buttons, zippers, cards, books.

Step one: comparing objects

Start by showing your young writers how to compare two objects. For example: *This stuffed rabbit is bigger than the mouse, and it has larger ears. How else are they different?* Hear children's responses. *Both stuffed animals are fuzzy and they both have feet. How else are they similar, the same?* Listen to several children's responses.

Distribute the pairs of objects and ask peer partners to set up for a knee-to-knee conference. In their conferences, they are to tell all the ways the objects are alike and all the ways they are different. Rove around to help and encourage, or gather a group who need extra help with the task.

Reassemble the class and hear the results of the conferences. Compliment the partners on their work.

Step two: brainstorming a list of pairs to compare

Begin the lesson with the children brainstorming a **list of pairs that are similar**. List a couple of entries to get them started. Many children will name the objects they used previously in the knee-to-knee conferences. Remind them of objects they saw on field trips they have taken or that they know from thematic studies they've done. Here is a list collected from a combination kindergarten and first-grade class:

- dog and cat
- gerbil and cat
- horse and cow
- nickel and quarter
- frog and toad
- *The Three Little Pigs* and *Goldilocks and The Three Bears*
- whales and fish
- skunks and raccoons
- manatees and people
- snake and worm
- ball and bat (Logic is not necessarily a definitive characteristic of kindergarten students.)
- doctor and dentist
- baseball and football

When the class list has ten or more entries, invite students to tell one reason the things are alike and one reason they are different. Write their responses on the board after each pair on the list. Compliment them on their work.

Step three: making a flip book

A flip book is an easily constructed, concrete aid for writing comparisons. It's small enough to fit a child's hand and easily carried in pockets. Children like to make these themselves after you show them how.

Materials: A flip book is made from an 8°" by 11" sheet of unlined paper, but use a larger sheet of construction paper, 11" by 14", for your demonstration.

Directions: Perform these folds in front of the students using the large paper. Go slowly and repeat the procedures.

A. Fold a sheet of unlined paper to look like a hot-dog roll.

B. Fold that down to look like a hamburger roll.

C. Fold that down again, to look like half a peanut butter sandwich.

D. Unfold the paper back to its hot-dog roll shape. Open the sheet part of the way and drape it over your arm, so it looks like a roof top.

E. Cut each fold line up one side only, to the top of the roof.

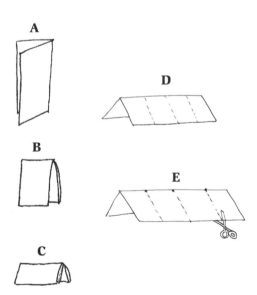

Using the flip book to make comparisons

Draw a flip book on the board as a **model**, or use your large one made of heavy paper. Talk about a pair that is not included in the class list. Compare them in terms of the attributes they share. Write about one of the pairs on a top flap of the booklet. Write about the second of the pair, comparing it to the first in terms of that same attribute, on the bottom flap. *Ducks have webbed feet. Chickens don't.*

Ducks have webbed feet.	Ducks quack.	Ducks swim.	Ducks lay eggs.
Chickens don't.	Chickens cluck.	Chickens don't.	Chickens do, too.

Point out to your students that you compared the duck and the chicken by looking at different attributes: feet, food, teeth, habitat, sound, size, what they do, color, etc. Invite the children to write about the pair they want to compare. You can let them copy your work (which is what happens after modeling) or not. You might allow them to copy your model the first time you do this lesson but then not in later ones.

Children should work in partnerships as they draw or write about the differences and similarities. You should encourage them to talk as they work.

Since it is an introduction lesson, children will not be good at the task. Encourage them, but plan to reiterate the lesson at a later date.

In later grades, developing writers can use this activity to practice paragraphs using the transition words that are specific to comparison writing. *A duck has a bill, **while** a chicken has a beak. **Unlike** the chicken, a duck has webbed feet. **Both** ducks and chickens lay eggs.*

Venn Diagrams

A Venn diagram is a graphic representation of the attributes of two (or three) entities, showing the ones they have in common and the ones they do not. It is an abstract organization scheme and, as such, is not useful for emergent writers as a technique to plan the presentation of their writing. It is useful, however, to show children how to record information and to develop organized thought. We can model Venn diagrams orally and concretely in the primary grades.

> *Materials:*
> * two large, plastic Hoola Hoops
> * a set of attribute cards for two things being compared — I use *dogs* and *cats*. Prepare some common attribute cards in advance of the lesson, and have extra blank ones ready for the attributes children will add.

> **The Model: Comparing a dog and a cat**
> Gather the class in a circle and label one Hoola Hoop for *cat* and one for *dog*. Show children the cards with attributes about cats and dogs. Ask them to think of more as you work. Write the ones they contribute on the extra cards with a marker. Invite students to put the cards in the appropriate Hoola Hoop after they read and consider them.

> **Teacher:** *Here's the first card: Bark. Which animal does that? Shall we put it in the dog's Hoola Hoop? Yes.*
> *Here's another card: Meow. Which animal does that? Sure, put it in the cat's Hoola Hoop.*

*Here is another card: Animal. Oh, a cat and a dog are both animals. What
shall we do with just one card? Let's overlap the cat's and dog's Hoola
Hoops so the part that is inside the overlap means both the cat and dog.
Move the hoops until they overlap.*

Now proceed with all the cards and place them in Cat, Dog, or Both.

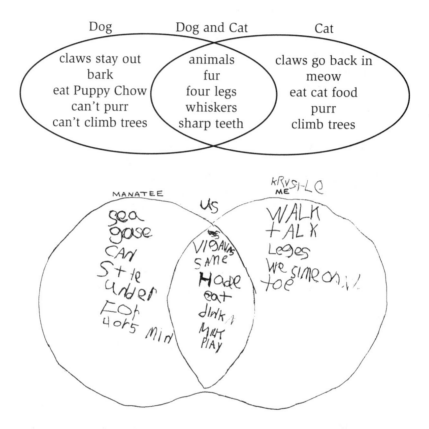

Dog	Dog and Cat	Cat
claws stay out	animals	claws go back in
bark	fur	meow
eat Puppy Chow	four legs	eat cat food
can't purr	whiskers	purr
can't climb trees	sharp teeth	climb trees

Many first graders will understand the concept of the overlapping or shared attributes.
Some will not. Children's brains mature at different rates.

Do not ask youngsters to use Venn Diagrams to organize their writing. Just model the
comparison concept for them. This is primarily a precursor activity for writing work they
will do as developing writers in later grades. Encourage children to use Venn diagrams to
organize information they learn through reading, pictures, TV, and observation.

Sorting and Clumping

When children are comfortable comparing animals, people, and objects, have them use
comparison to sort and group *objects*, and finally, to sort and classify concrete, *written
information*. Grouping or clumping concrete information is the basis for writing in the
expository genre. Paragraphing is the writing convention used to separate the clumps.

Model sorting for all your students. Have them practice comparing and sorting collections
of objects first. When they sort their objects, ask children to name the attributes they used
to make two piles. Your sorting model, using buttons and providing a reason for each
division, might go as follows:

*Some of the buttons have just two holes. They go together. Some of them have four
holes, and they go together. Or, I could put all the plastic ones in one pile and all the
metal ones in another.*

Give your students TV-dinner trays or compartmentalized, urethane food trays and have them sort **objects**: buttons, stones, sea shells, zippers, seeds, small toys, pasta. Ask them to explain their sorting schemes.

Next, show them how to sort **printed symbols** in the form of playing cards, ABC picture cards, game cards, geometric-shape cards, etc. This is more abstract than object sorting.

Finally, have them sort **pictures of objects** by various schemes, various attributes: size, color, weight, shape, texture, composition, and all kinds of features: stripes, polka dots, fringe.

Sorting and grouping is an important science skill as well as a writing skill. Have primary students sort and group often.

See and hear authors sorting and clumping

After lots of practice sorting or clumping, read a science Big Book to your class. Pre-read the book and see that the information is presented in clumps. For instance, a book about the ocean might have several pages with pictures of *sea mammals*, then a page or two about *fish*, a page or two about *plants*, a page or two about *sea birds*, a page or two about the *sea shore*. The information is presented in clumps, groups, or *categories*. Point that out to your students.

Read another informational book and ask them to find where the author presents new clumps of information. Many photo-illustrated science Big Books have a table of contents. Show young writers how authors help their readers by telling them about the clumps in the tables of content. This activity incorporates teaching about the parts of a non-fiction book.

A Precursor-to-paragraphing: Three Models

With practice in sorting objects and symbols, and in seeing how writers sort and arrange information, emergent writers in Stages Five through Seven, and most first- and second-grade students will be ready for the following exercise. Model this for all your writers, but do not ask early emergent writers to do this. They can watch and help when the other writers try it.

In the following three models, children will sort written information. The **first** model should use information they are all likely to know — I use *dogs* for the model topic. A **second** model should follow your teaching a two-week or longer science or social studies theme, with multi-media presentations, lots of reading, charts, a field trip, related art projects, i.e., total immersion. In this second model, the children will have common and similar bits of information. A **third** model should follow, with young writers picking a topic based on their personal expertise. Each writer will then be dealing with different information. Each model can be repeated any number of times before moving to the next one. The series of three should be presented during the course of a year.

Model One: Universal Topic

Materials:
- 10-12 strips of heavy, unlined paper or card stock, 3" by 16" (As you sort them you will attach them to the easel or board with clips or magnets in a long column — ladder-like.)
- large sheet of blank newsprint or printed newspaper
- glue sticks, paste, or masking tape
- markers

Procedure:

This model takes approximately 25 minutes. Do not use it as a starting component of your writing workshop unless you extend the session to include this model and a writing component. (In every daily writing workshop session children must have time for independent or guided writing.) Consider this a science activity, if you will, or critical-thinking development. It is all these things.

Gather your class at the easel. Hold up the science Big Book that you've used previously to show how the author used groups of pages for things that go together. Remind them of that concept: clumping related information — the things that go together are close together in the book. Show them a few pages to help them recall.

> **Teacher:** *Let me show you how authors get ready to write about stuff they know. We all probably know quite a bit about dogs. I am going to use that for our lesson today. What do we know about dogs?*

> **Children:** (Have them tell you what they know about dogs. Tell them to go slowly because you are going to write what they know.) *Dogs growl. Dogs eat dog food. Dogs chase cats. Dogs have sensitive ears. They eat Puppy Chow. They like people.*

Write each sentence on the consecutive strips of paper attached to the easel or black-board. As you see several categories of information emerge, encourage children to give more of the same kind of information. Prompt with: *What else do they eat? What else do dogs do? What else do they look like?* When you have a list of about 8-12 items, ask the children to read the list with you.

HELP

Ask your aide, if you have one, to write the sentence strips as you say them. Or, ask a fifth-grader to come to your room when you do this model. Or, prepare some easily anticipated sentences for the topic, and write the remainder during the model. Whatever you do, you will need 8-12 strips to continue the model.

Now have the children form a circle. You and your students will read the strips and decide how to sort them into three or four groups in the center of the circle. Have the children read the strips chorally as you present each one, and have helpers put them in the groups.

> **Teacher:** *Look at all this information we know about dogs. How shall we arrange it so the reader won't get confused? Let's see.* Hold up first strip and have children read it with you: *Dogs chase cats.* Place it on the floor in the center of the circle.

> **Teacher:** Read the next: *Dogs eat bones. Is this about what dogs do or what they eat? Eat. Then, we need a new pile.*

Dogs eat bones.

> **Teacher:** Read the next: *Dogs growl. Is this about what dogs do or what they eat? What they do. We need to put it with 'Dogs chase cats.'*

> **Teacher:** The next: *Dogs have sensitive ears. Is this about what they do or what they eat? No? It's about what they look like. We may need to start a new pile.*

Continue until you have used all the sentence strips: *Dogs have paws. Dogs eat dog biscuits. Some dogs are white and some dogs are brown.*

Extra strips

If there are one or two information strips that don't fit in any of the three to four groups, tell your writers it is all right to give them away to another writer or to throw them away. (Writers do not use all the information they know about a topic in one article or book.) Older children often want to retain the extra strips and will ask if they can get more information that will go with these unmatched facts to build another group. Yes, research. That is what adult writers do.

When the sorting is complete, have children help you paste or tape the strips in their groups on the large sheet of paper, leaving some space between groups and leaving some room at the top for a title. Hang the large piece of paper, and have the young writers read the clumps again. Ask for title suggestions. Write one on the top in marker.

The finished product is the paste-up. The writing will not be graceful and will not flow logically. There is no introduction or ending. There is no mention of indentation. No matter; we are concerned here only with children understanding the clumping principle.

Closing

Show them the Big Book again.

> **Teacher:** *See how the author of this book put all the stuff about animals on these two pages, then all the stuff about machines on these two pages, and then all the stuff about water on these two pages. We just did the same thing. This is what writers do.*

Model Two: Theme Topic

During the two or more weeks of immersion in a theme, have students write information sentence strips, one or two a day. Model how to write just one fact per strip. (This may consist of one or two sentences.) Place blank strips in a box for children to take as needed. Large manila envelopes, reinforced with masking tape, are good places for writers to keep their strips. Remind them to put their names or initials on the back of each strip.

You also can give young writers a large sheet of art paper with lines drawn horizontally every 2-3 inches. They can record information on each line. When they are finished, they can cut the paper into strips. For some children, storing this single paper may be easier than storing strips.

I prefer using the strips because children like the feel of them; they are handy for editing by ear; and children's inventorying urge is satisfied as they make fact collections.

Helping young writers gather information and record it

- Take dictation on strips for some writers.
- Write information on the board that they articulate after seeing a film or hearing a book. Give them time to copy those sentences to strips.
- Show them how to copy single sentences of information from books.
- Encourage them to get information from other people.
- Make time for them to read their strips to one another.
- Allow children to trade strips and share information.
- Have them practice reading the strips with feeling so they can edit them by ear for periods.
- Have them edit each other's strips for a capital letter at the beginning of the sentence(s).

Marilyn Cafaro, confirms that some of her first and second graders can independently write fact strips from what they see on films and TV programs related to the theme topic.

Sorting information

Set aside time in the last days of a theme period for young writers to spread out their strips and sort them into groups of information that goes together. Work with half the class at a time as they will need your help.

Do not expect these young children to group or arrange the strips in logical order. What they will have accomplished is concretely sorting information on a topic they know. This sorting and grouping introduces them to the concept of paragraphing.

Paste-up product

Provide each child with a large sheet of newspaper or construction paper. Show students how to put just a blob of glue at each end of the strips when they paste them in clumps. Show them how they can move a strip later if they want. The pasted clumps of information on a sheet of newsprint or newspaper with an added title is the finished product. Students do not need to re-copy the piece.

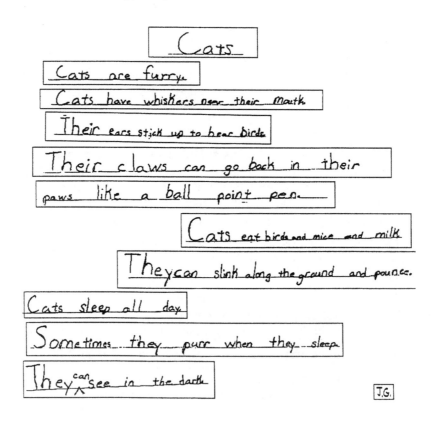

Model Three: Personal-expertise Topic

After the universal topic model and the theme model, it will be time for young writers to try this organizing technique on their own personal-expertise piece.

Start a daily writing workshop by showing children the pasted-up product from your first class model — mine was *Dogs*. Show some of their paste-up theme-information pieces. Tell them it is time for them to try this out using their personal expertise. Use that writer's vocabulary: *personal expertise*.

Ask children to recall or take out their list of things they know, places they have been, etc. that they made earlier in a pre-writing model (see Chapter 5). Ask them to choose something from their lists that they know well. Tell them you will do the same. Tell them they will have several days to work on this project.

Take the time to have children tell you and their classmates about their personal expertise. (Another opportunity for developing oral-language skills.) Write each child's topic on a card. Some will offer such topics as cats, iguanas, gerbils, and baseball. Some will copy each other's topic and some will complain: *He took mine. I was going to write about baseball.* Be prepared to show them two non-fiction books about the same topic. *See, many authors write about the same topic. But, each one writes it in her own special way.*

Modeling the list: Gathering your thoughts and your information

Demonstrate how to write your topic on the top of another list paper. My example: *Fishing.* Use a large strip of paper for all to see, an overhead transparency, or the blackboard. Thinking aloud, make a list of things you know about your topic.

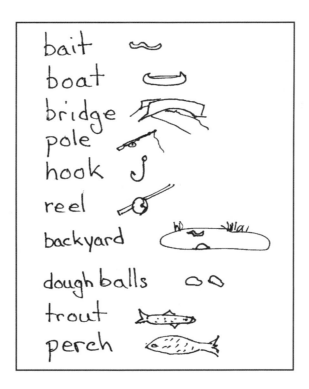

Invite young writers to hold knee-to-knee conferences to tell each other about their topics or to draw the things they will list. Then, have them construct their lists. This may take two days. They can take their lists home to work on them.

Modeling the sentence strips: a strip for each piece of information (one or two sentences about the same thing)

1. *You need worms to fish. I dig them in my garden.*
2. *You can fish from a boat. I like to fish from a bridge.*
3. *You need a pole, line, and hook.*
4. *I keep my worms in a plastic box.*
5. *You don't need a reel, but it helps.*
6. *I can fish in my backyard. I have a pond.*
7. *Dough balls are good if you can't find worms.*
8. *I like to catch trout and perch.*

Tell your young writers they will be writing a sentence strip for each of the things they know about their topic. Remind them where blank sentence strips are kept, to write their names on the back of their strips, and where to store them. Give each student a reinforced manila envelope.

ESOL and emergent writers in Stages Three and Four may copy your first model (*dogs*) or the theme model, especially if these are displayed in the room. If they use them for their personal-expertise piece, that's fine. They want to be involved in the project. They want to be writers.

Help children by taking dictation, guiding them in their writing, hearing some of the strips. Before the workshop is finished each day, have the children read their strips to each other. Encourage them to edit the strips by ear for periods at the ends of sentences. Students who are learning to write consistently with small letters also can edit for a capital letter to start each sentence.

Sorting time:

When writers have eight or more strips, help them sort these into groups of related information. Use your strips to model and review sorting and pasting for the group of children who are ready. The rest of the class will be writing or illustrating some of the strips, reading their strips in knee-to-knee conferences (*How does it sound? Is it interesting? Does it make sense?*), editing their sentence strips for periods in edit-by-ear conferences, editing each other's strips for a capital letter to start, or sitting with your group as a preview. You might enlist the help of fifth graders to work with one or two children at a time.

Invite young writers to make a title strip and to read their reports to other writers who are finished.

In a first-grade class, following this activity, I observed a young writer who finished his sorting and pasting quickly and declared, "I'm done." When he had read his piece to his partner, he gathered up extra strips and walked around the class telling writers he was the TITLE MAN, and asking, Do you want a title? Some took him up on his offer. Other children took dictation for each other and helped with pasting.

I observed a little girl who wrote on her strips: dogs can run. dogs can run. dogs are fun. dogs can run. dogs are fun. dogs are fun. dogs can run. She made 8 of them. Then she sorted them into two piles: dogs can run and dogs are fun. She competently pasted them on a large sheet of newsprint and added a title: Dogs. A classmate read it and said, They rhyme. The author smiled and read her piece to everyone, again and again. She understood the sorting concept. (She was an emergent writer in the inventorying stage.)

Your model:

Brainstorm associated words for your topic. Then write a set of strips for the topic. Store them in your writer's notebook or in an envelope, ready to use when you do this third model of sorting personal-expertise information. Tab this page to find it quickly.

TOPIC: _____
SENTENCES:

Highlights of paragraph precursor model:

The model and the associated activities are hands-on and concrete and are based on personal expertise. They incorporate science skills and set the stage for later writing in paragraphs. Additionally, the model reveals an important revision principle — you can move text. Some young writers will use the principle, moving a sentence strip from one group to another, saying, *Uh, oh, this really belongs in this group.* Praise them for doing this, for considering their readers.

Beginnings

The beginning of an expository piece lets readers know what the piece is about. Whatever form it takes, the first sentence or two must also intrigue, invite, and raise curiosity. This is called the hook. It can be written in so many forms — questions, exclamations, sentence fragments, alliterative words, riddles, a play on words, quotes, words in bold font, hyperbole, sounds.

Young writers can learn to write a variety of hooks. Encourage them to imitate the pros. Read articles to them from *Ranger Rick* or other children's magazines. Tab articles that start with a question hook. Question hooks are an easy introduction to the overall concept of hooks. *Hey, what are these elephants doing? Are they taking a shower?* begins one about elephant trunks. *What, you don't like crunch caterpillars on your pizza?* begins another about eating insects for their rich protein content.

Model question hooks for your students, using a picture as a prompt. For example, write about a picture of a manatee. Start with: *Have you ever seen a manatee up close?* or, *How big do you think a manatee is?* rather than, *This is about manatees.*

Manatees

Did you now manatees are endangered? Thay get hit by boates Prpeler. Oh No! And thay can Not breth under water. Thay swim Varey slowly!

Crane

Wie DiD Tis BeAr Yet The Fish? BYecus HY Was Hggry

Have your young writers practice hooks as a target skill. Later introduce the use of *exclamations* and *onomatopoeia* as hooks.

Your model: Find a picture you love. Write two or three sentences about the picture. Start with a question hook. Now, paste your picture on a large piece of drawing paper or on a sheet of greenbar paper and make a note here where you have filed it.

Hook model filed: _____.

Endings

Writers in the primary grades, and for that matter, any grade, often find endings are the hardest part of composing a piece.

Many children will simply stop when they get to the end of a page. If you tell them, *You don't have an ending*, they will point to the bottom of the page and say, *There's the end.* If you still don't get it, they will help you by writing, in large capital letters at the bottom of their work, THE END. While primary children cannot be expected to write well-developed beginnings or endings, they can end pieces in a simple and satisfying manner.

One effective way for them to end a piece is to use a statement about how they **feel** about the subject. They can write it in one or two sentences: *I like manatees. I want to pet one.* Model this type of ending for your students often. Make it a target skill. Additional endings second-graders can use are: make a comparison or use a universal word (all, every day, everyone, always, world, etc.).

Supporting Details in Opinion Papers

Essay deals with abstract concepts of ideas and argument and is properly addressed in grades four and higher. You can, however, as a precursor to essay writing in the later grades, introduce primary students to the concept of *supporting details* in opinion papers.

Children do have opinions, and we should encourage their voicing them. Teaching them the kinds of details writers use to support their opinions will help them understand that we cannot convince people of our ideas by simply repeating them or saying them louder. *Does too! Does not! Does too! Does not! ...*

Supporting details consist of concrete information. This is a concept young writers can understand and apply.

In an essay, a writer supports a thesis — an idea, opinion, or an argument — with various kinds of details. Among them are
- authoritative quotes (for the youngest writers this may be their grandmother, aunt, coach, teacher, mom, dad)
- proofs
- statistics (for the youngest writers this means numbers)
- descriptive details
- narrative vignettes (little stories)
- comparisons and analogies
- real-life examples
- scientific facts
- graphics: diagrams, tables, graphs, maps
- definitions
- allusions
- self-evident truths

Young writers understand and can use several of these kinds of supporting details. The easiest for them are **descriptive details, proofs, numbers, comparisons, quotes, and graphics.**

The first opinion paper model

I introduce the concept of supporting details to young writers who write more than two sentences by asking them to tell me something they are good at. I write one of their statements on the board. *I am good at dancing.* I tell the child who contributed the statement that that is his opinion and not everyone might agree or believe him. *How can you prove it?* I ask.

Some typical answers are: *I just am. I dance all the time. I danced at a recital. I love to dance. My mom says so. I know how to dance.* Write all the **proofs** on the board. Ask the class which ones they think prove the dancer is good at it. With discussion, they should arrive at a consensus: *I danced at a recital*, and *My mom says so.* Compliment them on choosing good proofs.

Now ask students to write an opinion, *I am good at......* on their papers. Do one of your own on the easel or board. Have children read their **opinion statements** to one another. Invite several students to tell what their partners wrote. Next, ask children how they will **prove it.** Model with yours.

> Write a statement of opinion such as, *I am good at quilting.* Then, write a detail that **proves it.** *I am good at quilting. I can make a quilt fast, in a month.*

Call on writing partners to tell what **proofs** they heard. They may claim to have won a prize, played on a team, had their work displayed in the school, not gotten hurt doing the activity. These are great. They may say they like what they are good at or where they do it. Receive everything, except repeating the statement, as proof. Most of your class will not be good at this. Their proofs may not really be proofs. (Young writers will need many more models, in each subsequent grade, to come up with the substantial proofs they will need to support an expository thesis in high school, college, or on-the-job writing.)

In a subsequent model, add a sentence to your model to introduce the **authoritative quote** (who else says so).

> *I am good at quilting. I can make a quilt fast, in a month. My husband says my quilts are beautiful.*

Later, model the use of **a number, a graphic**, and a **comparison**. Demonstrate them separately. When children can use each kind of supporting detail in a two-sentence opinion paper, encourage them to try for two or three in one paper. Present the series about supporting details during the year and repeat the models often.

Move the sentences around within the model paragraph to show children how one sentence might be the best last sentence. This helps develop their ear for expository writing.

> *I am good at quilting. I can make a quilt in a month. I've made 40 quilts. I like to make patchwork quilts best. This is a patchwork quilt (drawing of a quilt patch with labels of border, stitching, name of pattern). My husband says my quilts are beautiful.*

Your model: Tab this page to find your model quickly when you present this lesson.

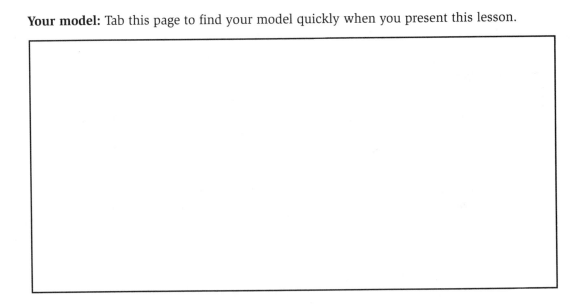

Help those children who can write these opinion papers to find topics. Ask them, *What do you think about...? How do you feel about...?* Use children's picture books that illustrate voicing opinions. Read:

Mine's The Best, by Crosby Bonsall (HarperCollins)
Will I Have a Friend, by Miriam Cohen (MacMillan Pub.)
It's Much Too Hot, by Bob Graham (Gallery Books)

Literature-response Writing

Writing about Books

Literature response is expository writing, whether the literature we respond to is narrative or expository. We *locate information;* we *tell what we learned;* we *explain* how the piece relates to ourselves; we *compare* characters to one another and to ourselves; we *locate* the story in time and space; we *identify* the plot. Writing about literature provides a link from reading to expository writing that we can develop in our daily writing workshop.

The first literature-response work for primary children should be oral and based on concrete facts. After reading a book to your class, ask questions. About an information book: *Where does the author tell about the pictures? What is this book about? What did we learn? In what part of the book did we learn that?* About a story: *Who are the main characters? Where are they, inside or out? In the county? In the city? What does the main character want? How did she get it?*

<table>
<tr>
<td>

³/H
The Tale Of Johnny Town Mouse
Beatrix Potter
Timmy Willie doesn't
like the town. Afraid of everthing.
He was nervouse in the hamper
In longs to be back home

</td>
<td>

Page 15   He awoke in fright
              trembled
Page 16 dogs barked. · · · ·
21 T.W almost fright
33 The noise upstairs made scared. · · ·
34 appetite failed. · · ·
34 fell faint
44 grew thin

</td>
</tr>
</table>

Analyzing literature for its organization is difficult. It is not something primary students write about. But, many young writers can recognize and *tell* you that an information book is organized using ABC order or by clumping information together. They often are able to identify the basic plot in fiction.

Plots can be sorted into five basic categories. When you read a story to your class, talk about the kind of plot it has. Have children tell you what plots they hear in stories or see on TV. Use primary children's language when you make a chart of plots.

- lost and found
- good guys vs. bad guys
- character has a problem and solves it, or wants something and gets it at the end
- mystery, and the main character solves it
- character is in a storm or something scary in nature, and lives through it

Flip Books

Written literature response can start with making comparisons between two books. Using a flip book (see page 99, this chapter) is an excellent way for first and second graders to respond. It is a hands-on activity, the writing is short, and the concept is simple. Young writers can compare books by their pictures, contents, information, maps, diagrams, characters, setting, etc.

This book has photographs, this one has drawings.
This book has people in it, this one has animals.
This story happens on a farm, this story happens in the city.

Story Frames

Young writers can respond to literature by using a prepared graphic organizer. Children draw components of the story and write a sentence or two about them. These organizers are called story frames. Most include the basic story components: character(s), setting, character's problem, what happened, and the problem solution.

When young writers can use these frames with ease, some begin to use them as a planning device for their own stories. They are akin to storyboards, a graphic planner that requires the writer to draw the sequence of scenes he envisions for his story. This kind of graphic planner is useful only to the child who understands chronological order, usually a late first-grade or second-grade development.

Summarizing, when done properly, is a highly analytical process and is impossible for young writers. I would not recommend asking children to attempt it in the primary grades. They will usually try to retell the story, scene by scene, which is not summary. Stick to literature responses that deal with concrete facts about the book. *What does the author tell about whales eating? Where does the story happen?*

Chapter 14
Personal Narrative

Narrative writing is story writing — about people and events. Narratives can be imaginary or true. Narration **is characterized by the passage of time** and **is organized chronologically**. It is enriched with descriptive writing, literary devices, and facts. It can be told in the first person or third, in the present tense or past.

Personal narrative writing should follow personal, informational expository in your writing program. This continues children's control over the content of their writing; they are writing about their own experiences, the events and stories in their lives. In personal informational narrative, they are writing about what they know. Use personal narratives to teach the basic characteristics and techniques or the narrative genre. Only when most of your young writers have demonstrated facility with these skills, should you venture into fictional narrative (see discussion in the following section).

Developing an Ear for Personal Narrative

An imbalance in our read-aloud practices develops children's ear for *fictional* narrative. This imbalance is initiated by parents reading bed-time stories to children. It is reinforced by teachers choosing fiction as the predominant read-aloud genre. In addition, emergent-reader series are usually based on fictional stories. (We might say, *Children love stories*, to defend this imbalance, but psychologists have found that it doesn't matter what you read to children; what they love is to be held on your lap and have you read to them. They will ask for the same book, again and again, loving the ritual, the sound of your voice, the coziness of it. You could read from the newspaper, and they would love it just as much.)

Is it any wonder that youngsters think fictional stories are the most important? By first grade, in response to this continued imbalance in our read-aloud choices, and our use of the word *story* when we refer to children's writing, their natural inclination toward expository loses ground and *story* starts to dominate their writing. While this is fun for some exceptionally imaginative children, it is not the genre of writing that will best support them academically.

For many children, fiction writing is not fun. Fiction is a difficult genre. It is particularly so for primary children, most of whom do not have a well-developed concept of sequence. Young writers — mainly girls who break the code early and become avid readers — often become disenchanted with writing in elementary school because they see that their stories do not measure up to the standards of the books they read. We can avoid this disenchantment if we introduce and encourage *personal and informational narrative* writing before fiction.

> Support the children who write fiction naturally with lessons about that genre. Many gifted children who are good readers fall in this category. Help them be the best they can be. But, if and when you see indications of dissatisfaction creeping into their attitude toward their writing, steer them back to personal informational expository and personal narrative where their unique experience will set their writing apart from their reading material.

Literature Models

Children's picture books written in the first person make good models for personal narrative writing. These first-person stories are not true personal narrative writing because they are not authored by a child, but are written as if they were. I call them Sound-Alike Personal Narratives. They are stories that do not have plots of the problem-and-solution type common to most fiction. Some examples are:

Bonsall, Crosby. *The Day I Had to Play With My Sister*. New York: HarperCollins Publishing Co., 1972.

Bunting, Eve. *Our Teacher is Having a Baby*. Boston: Houghton Mifflin Co., 1992.

Curtis, Jamie Lee. *Tell Me Again About The Night I Was Born*. New York: HarperCollins Publishing Co., 1996.

Howard, Elizabeth Fitzgerald. *The Train to Lulu's*. New York: Bradbury Press, 1988. (Reading Rainbow)

Kellogg, Steven. *I Was Born About 10,000 Years Ago*. New York: William Morrow and Co., 1996.

Kellogg, Steven. *Best Friends*. New York: Dial Book for Young Readers, 1986.

Lessac, Frane. *My Little Island*. New York: HarperCollins Publishing, Co., 1984. (Reading Rainbow)

Meyer, Mercer. *I*. New York: Dial., 1968.

O'Donnell, Elizabeth Lee. *I Can't Get My Turtle to Move*. New York: William Morrow and Co., 1989.

Rockwell, Anne. *The Storm*. New York: Hyperion Books for Children, 1994.

Rosenberg, Liz. *The Carousel*. New York: Harcourt Brace and Co., 1995.(Reading Rainbow)

Rylant, Cynthia. *The Relatives Came*. New York: Dutton, 1985.

Rylant, Cynthia. *When I Was Young in the Mountains*. New York: Dutton, 1982.

Stevenson, Robert Louis. *My Shadow*. New York: G.T. Putnam, Inc., 1990.

Wyeth, Sharon Dennis. *Always My Dad*. New York: Alfred A. Knopf, 1995. (Reading Rainbow)

Yolen, Jane. *All Those Secrets of the World*. New York: Little, Brown and Company, 1991. (Reading Rainbow)

Organization

Young writers' first narratives are based on personal experience and are informational in nature. They are not stories in the true sense, with beginnings, a focused middle, and an ending. Children may use the past tense and tell us something they did, or something they discovered. But before they write true stories, they need some facility with time sequence.

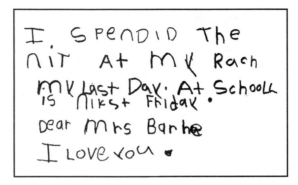

I SPENDID The
nit At MY Rach
my Last Day. At SchooL
is first Friday.
Dear Mrs Barhe
I Love You

Emergent writers do not organize their first narratives chronologically. These young writers tell the most important thing first, and they tell events in the order in which they remember them. *I threw up at the mall,* a child will announce on a Monday morning in Show and Tell, or in writing workshop. When we get the whole story, we find out more about what led to the event or what happened later. *I felt sick. My mom was mad.*

Past tense

When children develop an ear for story as a result of our read-aloud program, or they come to school from a background where reading aloud is a ritual, they may begin to write stories in response to some of their drawings and pictures. Some will understand past tense and tell what happened in their pictures or they will mix tenses, using them indiscriminately. This mixture of present and past tense continues until children understand sequence. Do not try to correct it until they do.

Sequence and time transitions

When youngsters tell stories, we encourage sequencing by prompting them, *And then what happened?* We also encourage sequencing by reading a story to them and asking them to retell it. And finally, we encourage sequencing when we model a sequence of events in our own writing. Some children may begin to understand time sequence in late kindergarten, and most children can relate events in chronological order by the end of second grade.

Soon children may begin to use *And then* ... repetitively, to hold our attention when they tell us stories from their lives. They usually hold onto our arms or sleeves as well, not wanting us to escape before they are finished. This natural story-telling technique, *And then*, appears in their writing. And then, we go bananas when we see it.

Use the appearance of *and then* in young writers' stories as a signal that they are ready for a lesson in narrative time transitions, replacing the *And thens* with words such as *Later, Soon, After that, Suddenly, On Sunday*. (See time transition lesson in the following subsection.)

The Shape of a Personal Narrative

Personal narratives are characterized by their shape, that is, by the percentage of writing devoted to the beginning, the middle, and the end. A personal narrative looks like a *snake that ate a rat,* or a bell curve.

The All-important Middle

The middle of a personal narrative is its **focus**. This is an important criterion for scoring narratives in prompted writing assessments. The concept should be introduced when children start to write personal narratives. The middle of the narrative, the focus, should contain the most writing, the most details, the most information. Thus, the snake-that-ate-the-rat analogy.

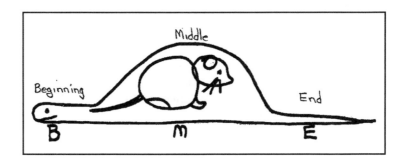

Draw this picture for young writers when you introduce personal narratives. Label it as shown, with B for beginning, M for middle, and E for end. The snake's belly, with the rat inside, is the biggest, most exciting part for the snake and the rat, and for the story as well. (Sequence facility is a prerequisite for young writers to write stories, but emergent writers in the pre-sequence stage can benefit from hearing this lesson as a preview.)

Marilyn Cafaro's first and second graders have changed the rat to mouse for their model. "Mouse for Middle," they told me. When they work on personal narratives, they draw a small snake with the bulge of a mouse at the top of each page to remind them of a story's parts. The last time I visited their class, they showed me how they had refined it further by drawing a little hook at the snake's mouth.

Young writers can hear the focus in each other's personal narratives and can give a thumbs-up signal when writers share their stories. They like referring to the main event, the middle of the story, as the **rat or mouse**.

When I introduce focus to young writers, I ask them to tell me of any trips they have taken or adventures they have had. I urge them to tell me what was the best part of those trips, adventures, or events. *Don't tell me all about the car trip and how you were bored — I'll be bored too*, I say, *Tell me about the very best part. Tell me everything about it that made it the best part.*

Advise your students that most of their writing should be about the exciting part of their story - the RAT. Give them the opportunity to talk to a partner about the best part, the middle of their narrative.

The details comprising the middle of most children's first personal narratives will be presented in a rather list-like fashion. As they learn time sequence, they will start to present them chronologically, usually employing the word *then* or *and then*. Both these writing behaviors, list-like details and the use of *then*, are normal and developmental. Show them how to make lists of single words about the exciting part of the story to write sentences.

Make writing detailed sentences about the most exciting part a target skill. Start with one detail, and progress to three in the course of the year. Specific targets are sentences that tell *how, why, how many, which one, what kind*, or *more of what happened*. Descriptive-attribute target skills can be added as well.

Model: adding each kind of detail, one at a time.

My dad took me fishing.

Add the target skill: what else happened?
My dad took me fishing. I caught three fish and Dad caught one.

Add the target skill: how?
My dad took me fishing. I caught three fish and Dad caught one. We used worms for bait.

Add the target skill: what kind?

My dad took me fishing. I caught three fish and Dad caught one. They were big bass.

The Beginning

The beginning of a story tells the reader *who, what, when,* and *where*: the journalistic four Ws. A personal narrative starts with these elements, then takes the reader quickly to the *rat*, the middle.

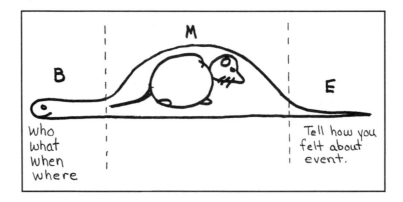

At the mouth and head of the Snake-That-Ate-a-Rat drawing, I write *who, what, where, and when.* That's the start of the tale. A one-sentence beginning to a personal narrative is perfectly acceptable for young writers.

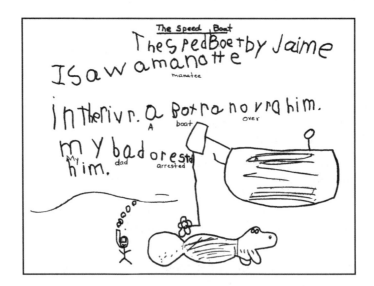

A first grader's writing might begin like this:
I went to the zoo with my mom.

Introduce the target skills of *when* and *where* separately:
I went to the zoo with my mom on Saturday.
My dad took me fishing to a pond.
We went to the mall last night.

Next show children how they can add both *when* and *where* to the same sentence.
Yesterday my dad took me fishing on a pond.

Make *when* and *where* the target skills for personal narrative. Point out the *when* and *where* that authors have used when you read narratives to children. Give young writers

WHEN and WHERE cards to hold up during read-aloud time, Author's Chair, and peer conferences to indicate that they recognize when authors use those details.

The Ending

Primary-grade children are very literal. When you tell them they have no ending, they will show you where their writing stops and tell you that is the end. In case you still do not get it, they will write, THE END after the last word.

Avoid this confusion, and teach them some strategies for ending a personal story. A good ending for young writers to use in their personal narratives is to tell:

- how they felt about the exciting part
- what they learned from the experience
- what was accomplished

The tail of the tale is small, as in the drawing of the snake-that-ate-a-rat. One sentence will suffice for young writers.

> A Pig Kissed Me.
> When We Went to
> Honsatr Fram's A Pot belly
> Pig Kissed My Knee.
> Dockousding. *Disgusting*

A kindergarten student used a one-word ending effectively.

Model the target-skill ending: *tell how you felt at the end of an event*. This is the easiest one for young writers. When they have achieved success with that ending, introduce them to another.

> *My dad took me fishing to a pond yesterday.*
> *I caught three fish and Dad caught one.*
> *They were bass. I like fishing.*
> (Or: *I learned how to bait a hook*. Or: *We caught fish for supper*.)

Transitions: Getting Rid of *And then*

When your primary students' personal narratives abound with *And thens*, you can help them become more graceful writers.

At the start of a daily writing workshop, read a short narrative you prepared containing several *And thens*. Then, read it back to your writers, substituting words such as *Later, Soon, Suddenly*, or *The next day* for the 'And thens'. Next, share a narrative Big Book that contains at least two time transitions. Read the story with the children. Stop when you get to a time transition and point it out to the children. *See how this author used 'Later' instead of 'And Then?'* Invite children to try this when they write.

On another day, as a starting component, invite children to find *And then*, and *Then* in their own narratives. Children can read their work to a peer in a knee-to-knee conference. Ask for volunteers who found some *And thens*. Praise them for finding them. Ask them to read their pieces to the class in Author's Chair. When they get to an *And then*, ask them what other word they would like to use. They can ask other children for ideas.

Model at the easel or blackboard how to cross out an *And then* and write one of the *time words*. Do not expect that young writers will select the most appropriate time transitions the first time they do this. One young writer wrote:

I got up. Later I ate cereal. Suddenly I played baseball with my friends.

The young writer has the right idea.

Your model: Make up a four to five sentence narrative about what you did from the time you got up until you got to school. Use *And then* at the start of every sentence. Model how to cross these out and replace them with time words. Write those words next to this model. Tab this page to find it quickly.

Lessons and Models for Personal Narratives

How Did You Feel?

If a target skill for ending a personal narrative is to tell how they feel, then children need more words than *happy, glad, sad,* and *mad*. Brainstorm vocabulary about feelings to make a class chart. When you read to students, point out words that tell feelings.

Happy: *glad, joyful, excited, cheery, amused, cozy, safe, ...*
Sad: *hurt, teary, lonely, miserable, unhappy, ...*
Mad: *angry, furious, annoyed, irritated, ...*
Scared: *afraid, helpless, confused, ...*
Others: *proud, trusted, sorry, foolish, embarrassed, ...*

Have some volunteers **tell** how they felt about the central events in their narratives. Ask some to write how they felt about events or actions of people in their personal narratives. Show young writers how to add how they felt at the end of their stories.

What Did I Learn?

Many personal narratives are about events or actions that helped us learn something. Ask young writers to share a personal event in which they learned something about themselves.

- they are afraid of heights
- they sunburn very easily
- they are squeamish about baiting a hook
- they hate broccoli

Or, in which they learned to do something:
- sing a song
- jump rope
- fish
- swim
- ice a cake
- ride a two-wheel bike
- box
- use a computer
- cook

Model a personal narrative for them that tells what you learned.

I got a new bike. My mom ran beside me. Then she let go. I didn't know it. I rode by myself. That's how I learned to ride my bike.

Your model: Write a short personal narrative in which you learned something. Tab this page to find it quickly.

Informational Narrative

Many children exhibit an unquenchable thirst for facts and begin their quest to satisfy that need for knowledge as soon as they can read and write. Encourage them to write about factual information. They can do it in the narrative mode as well as expository.

Read non-fiction or informational narratives to young writers

Show young writers by example that not all *stories* have a plot and that some of them can be filled with factual information. *Ranger Rick* magazine usually features a piece like this each month. In it, the author might take the reader on a trip and provide facts about the topic as the trip progresses. Here is a short bibliography of picture books for primary children using that approach.

Cole, Joanna. *The Magic School Bus Inside a Bee Hive*. New York: Scholastic Press, 1991. (all the Magic School Bus books)

Culberson, Brenda Z. *Spoonbill Swamp*. New York: Henry Holt and Co. 1992.

Gibbons, Gail. *Say Woof: The Day of a Country Veterinarian*. New York: Macmillan Publishing Co. 1997.

Howlett, Bud. *I'm New Here*. Boston: Houghton Mifflin Co. 1993.

Magorian, Michelle. *Who's Going to Take Care Of Me?* New York: HarperCollins Publisher, 1990.

Mayfair, Linda Lee. *I Want to be a Fire Fighter.* New York: Sesame Street/Golden Books, 1991.

Pecher, Alese and Morton. *What's in the Deep?* Washington, DC: Acropolis Books, LTD. 1989.

Where or how I learned that fact

A narrative about a field trip, an adventure, an event, a place, or a person can tell how the writer learned a fact. A *How I Learned* _____ book appeals to fact gatherers.

Photo-prompted Personal Narratives

Take pictures of your class during field trips or at special school activities. Have the children write the story that goes with a photo in which they appear. Select target skills for them to consider as they write. Some target skills might be:

- use people's names
- tell what is happening in the photo
- tell what one of the people said
- use a number word
- make a comparison
- tell what you liked best about the event in the photo (as the ending)

Marilyn Cafaro takes pictures of her first and second graders all year long. She snaps away during every event, project, visit, field trip, and holiday. As a special Mother's Day project, children tape several pictures in which they are featured to greenbar paper, and then they write small stories about the events. They revise and edit them with their peers' and Cafaro's help. When the stories are edited, they pull the photos from their drafts, paste them on pages of a blank hand-publishing book, and copy their text in pencil to the pages. The book becomes their Mother's Day gift. The project takes about three weeks.

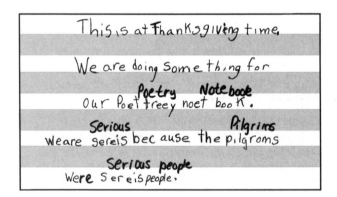

Poetry

Poetry in the primary grades should be an exclusively aural or oral exercise. Children should hear, perform, memorize, and recite poems. Poetry is meant to be heard. The language of poetry is rhythmical, lyrical, melodious; the sound of language is a large part of a poem's message.

Enjoy poetry to the fullest with primary students, but don't attempt to teach them its forms and structure. Don't require that they write poems.

Poetry instruction at this level should focus on the sound of words, feelings, imagery, and action. Poems tell a story, tell about people doing things, or invite us to wonder about life. Read both narrative and expository poetry to children.

Table-top Performance

Invite primary students to recite or read their favorite poems standing on the top of a table, as if it were a stage. Create a class collection of favorite, short poems printed on laminated cards. The children can copy other poems from books and magazines as well. Each week, several can take turns reciting from the table top.

I am convinced that we do not take sufficient advantage of young children's ability to memorize. Used wisely, memorization is a powerful learning tool. The things we learn as children stay with us forever.

Keep a collection of poetry in your classroom library, and read to your students often. Keep laminated copies of small poems in a container in your reading corner. Encourage children to recite them to each other. Poetry, with its rich vocabulary, rhythm, and meter, is easy to memorize and will develop children's ear for language.

Rhyme Lists

Here is another listing activity. For fun and practice, have young writers list words that rhyme. The urge to inventory is satisfied, and it is an easy task. Word families are reinforced. Introduce the list-making with some simple ditties: *One, two, buckle my shoe. Three, four, shut the door.* Model a list for emergent writers. Examples: *pink, ink, think, wink, sink.*

Your model list of rhyming words: Tab this page to find it quickly.

Fiction

If children choose to write fiction in their independent writing, support them with some basic genre and composing skills appropriate for their age and writing experience. Most primary students can understand and identify the fiction elements of characters and setting. Some can recognize the basic plots.

When you read fiction to children, help them identify characters, tell where and when the story takes place, and what the main character wants. Children need to know these elements if you expect or encourage them to write literature responses. When they learn the elements concurrently in writing, their knowledge of fiction structure is reinforced.

For your information:

Fiction is constructed from the following components:
- characters: major and minor; the techniques of character development
- setting: time, place, mood, and atmosphere
- plot: six basic plots with setbacks and tension-building devices
- point of view: first person, third person
- hooks: dialogue, action, setting, sounds, description of the main character, ...
- literary devices: alliteration, anthropomorphism (animals acting like people), hyperbole, onomatopoeia, simile, personification

Select the elements are appropriate to teach your fiction-writing students.

Lessons and Models for Fiction

Discuss Settings

Read literature examples that contain setting descriptions that invoke all the senses. Have students name the setting described. Besides children's literature, read from young writers' hand-published books. Doing so indicates that you value their work. Encourage young writers to tell where their stories take place.

Mini-lesson About Plots

Talk about the basic plots with students when you read fiction to them. Introduce each one with an example from their reading or movie background.

Examples:
- Lost and Found is the plot of *Hansel and Gretel*.
- Character vs. Nature is the plot of *Abel's Island*. (William Steig)
- Character with Problem is the plot of *Sylvester and the Magic Pebble*. (William Steig)
- Good guys vs. Bad guys is the plot of *The Three Little Pigs*.
- Crime/mystery and Solution is the plot of *The Case of the Hungry Stranger*. (Crosby Bonsall)
- Boy Meets Girl is the plot of *Cinderella*.

When children write imaginative stories, remind them to tell what the character's problem is and how the character solves it.

Setbacks in the Plot

Young writers usually do not write stories with well-developed plots. In second grade you can introduce the concept of setbacks to children who are comfortable writing imaginative fiction. A setback is an event that prevents the main character from immediately reaching his goal. The setback creates tension. Without setbacks, there is no story, at least not one that's of any interest to readers.

In well-developed fiction, there are often three or more setbacks. The series makes up the *middle* of the story. The main character overcomes each successive setback — the last one in a grand way that brings the story to a satisfactory close. Second graders are capable of understanding the concept and, in a simple way, can make up setbacks for their own stories.

Tell your young writers a really dumb story with no setbacks. Be sure to say it with feeling as if you think it is a really great story. For example:

> *Once upon a time there was a kid who lived in Iowa. One day he saw a beautiful palomino pony at the fair. He wanted the pony so badly. He asked his mother, "Will you get me that pony?" She said yes. He got his pony and was so happy.*

Wait. Watch their reaction. Ask them what they think of the story. Agree with them that it stinks. Then tell them a new version.

> *Once upon a time there was the kid who lived in Iowa. One day he saw a beautiful palomino pony at the fair. He wanted the pony so badly. He asked his mother, "Will you get me that pony." She said no. Next, he told his grandfather that, if he would buy him a pony, it could count for five birthdays. Grandfather said no. Then Grandfather said, "If you will work and raise the money for the pony this summer, I will buy the saddle and feed, and will let you keep it in my barn." The kid worked hard all summer, picking berries, selling worms, collecting eggs, shoveling manure, and helping with mowing, until he had enough money. He and grandfather went to buy the pony. The boy was so happy, but too tired to ride. (Pause) I'm just kidding..*

Now ask the students what they thought of the story. Which of the two stories did they prefer? Ask them to identify the setbacks the kid faced: Mom's no, Grandfather's no, Grandfather's challenge to raise the money on his own.

Ask students to find evidence of setbacks in the stories you read to them and the stories they read themselves. A list of setbacks might include injury, weather, losses, mistakes, misunderstandings, and mishaps. Some examples are:

- getting lost
- losing something
- getting hurt
- getting captured

Suggest to your second-grade writers that they each create a setback as a target skill for their next story and identify each other's in peer conferences.

Summary

Help your young writers find engaging writing topics in their personal lives. Value their personal expertise and experience. Encourage their natural inclination to write about what they know and feel by showing them the characteristics of the informational expository and personal narrative genres through modeled writing. Teach them the skills and techniques they need to make their personal stories interesting. Support their application of target skills when you read to them by illustrating how authors use these same skills. Primary children can be taught to write effectively. Believe in them.

Chapter 15
Composing and Literary Skills

When I teach young writers about composing skills, I call them *Tricks of The Trade.* These are the techniques writers use to make writing interesting, fun to read, and easy to understand. They include such things as varying sentence length and form, and using literary devices and specificity.

Examples of these techniques abound in children's literature, both fiction and non-fiction. Choose the ones that make appropriate target skills for your writers, and teach these skills through modeling. You can introduce them into your daily writing workshop as a whole-class starting component or to groups of writers who are ready for the skills.

Lessons and Models

Concept of Sentence

Before young writers can vary the length and form of sentences they must be sure of the concept of sentence. As discussed in Chapter 9, *visual* editing for complete sentences is difficult for young children because they are so literal. They equate the end of a sentence with the end of a line. Nor does analysis of sentences for subject and predicate work at this level.

The best way to teach the concept of complete sentences is to use children's natural syntactical knowledge of their native language. Help them hear sentences. (If that is not standard English, you will have to model often for these students.) Sharing sentence strips, editing by ear, choral reading, and your dictation procedure will reinforce the concept of sentence.

Expanding Sentences

This sentence has five words. Here are five more words. Five-word sentences are fine. But several together become monotonous. Listen to what is happening. The writing is getting boring. The sound of it drones. It's like a stuck record.

By this clever little essay, in his classic writer's guide, *100 Ways To Improve Your Writing,* Gary Provost[1] shows us why writers need to vary sentence length.

Emergent writers in Stages Six and Seven, and in all primary grades beyond these stages, can learn expansion techniques to revise their four-word sentences.

> *I have a dog. He likes to run. He plays with me.*

Model how to add details to sentences by answering some of the questions your readers might ask: *where, when, which one, how,* and *why. Where* or *when* are the easiest details for primary writers to add.

> Add *where* or *when.*
> *I have a dog. He likes to run in the park. He plays with me every day after supper.*

---

[1]Gary Provost, *100 Ways to Improve Your Writing,* (New American Library: New York, 1985), 61

Point out to young writers that not only is this less boring to read, but it is more informative and interesting.

Room to revise: Remember, you must model how to add to an existing manuscript. Show children how to use the ^, to write on the skipped lines, or add at the end. Most young writers will only add at the end unless they have seen models showing otherwise.

It is crucial to model additive revision in the primary grades if we want them to revise later on. Third graders are notorious for not wanting to mess up their papers, and fourth and fifth graders are notorious for writing on every line in small, tight script. There are two rules you can rely on: No room, no revision; Never done it, won't do it.

We train our students to do everything neatly, not to make mistakes. So they think, *Now you want me to mess up my paper with this extra sentence I have to add in here?* We need to teach them to regard most of their writing as work-in-progress, and to recognize the extra care it takes to prepare a piece for publication.

Your model: Write one or two sentences (personal expository preferred) that cry for a *when* or *where*. Create some for *how* and *why* as well. Tab this page to find it quickly when you are ready to model expanding sentences for your primary writers.

Specificity

One of the joys of reading is recognizing the familiar — being able to say *That is just like me; I do that, too; I've been there.* This joy is not reserved for adult readers. Young children smile when you read from a book in which the author has mentioned something they've felt, a place they've been, a game they play, a food they eat.

It is an author's job to give his readers that joy. **Specificity** is the means to do it. Instead of writing *store*, write *Home Depot*. Instead of writing *game*, write *Mother, May I*. Instead of writing *cereal*, write *Fruitloops®*.

Introduce this concept to your youngsters by playing the **General-to-Specific Game**. You can play this as a sit-and-stand game. Start with everyone sitting and when young writers give a correct response, have them stand. If you do the opposite, "*Wrong, sit down,*" you are accentuating the negative. Instead, accentuate the positive. Reward a correct answer, instead of penalizing children for an incorrect one.

Explain the game to the children with several examples. *If I say cereal, I want you to tell me a specific cereal, such as, Fruitloops® or Cheerios®.* Invite children to add more specific cereals to that list. *If I say flower, I would like you to tell me a specific flower, such as rose or tulip.* Again, have them practice this as an oral exercise.

Your Game Preparation

Prepare a list of general nouns and your list of specifics. I have started a list for you.

General	Specific
Cereal	Cheerios®, Rice Crispies®, oatmeal
Tree	apple, pine, oak, maple, orange
Flower	daisy, tulip, rose, lily

Next, play the game with the children, writing a specific example for each general term. Repeat, and have the young writers make a list of as many specific examples as they can think of for each general category.

Model specificity for your students. As you write in front of them, think aloud, and revise to specificity in your model. Example: *My dog is not feeling well. I think I have to take him to the veterinarian in town. Oh, my readers might like to know which town.* Cross out town. *I am going to change it to Bennington, where I live. And why don't I tell what kind of dog I have?* Cross out dog. *I am changing dog to poodle.*

Your model: Showing specificity revision: Tab this page to find it quickly when you are ready to model revision for specificity.

Don't Hit Your Reader Over the Head

Another joy of reading is figuring things out for yourself, using the author's clues. Providing those clues is one of the joys of writing. Show primary-grade writers who are beyond Stage Six how to do this. Share with them the concept of *not hitting their readers over the head with information.*

a) Write the following on the board or overhead projector.

> *I went swimming. It was fun.*

Read the sentences with the students. Orally and physically punctuate the second sentence with a BOING, tapping yourself lightly on the top of your head with the heel of your hand. Invite them to mimic the gesture. Can they picture what was fun? The reader has no fun figuring out if or why the swimming was *fun*. This kind of writing is called **hitting your reader over the head.**

b) Erase or cross out *It was fun*. Ask the students to provide information about swimming that would have made it fun. Write their information after the first sentence.

Example:

> *I went swimming. I got to dive off the board. My mom let me use her raft.*

c) Invite the students to try this technique with the sentences: *I have a dog. He is mean.* Ask the students to say *BOING* and tap themselves on the head when they read, *He is mean.*

The Nelsons have a dog. ~~He is mean.~~
He rips your socks. and he eats your shoes.
He will trie to bite you.
He will eat your Home work.
He is a mean dog to do that.

＊Hit on the head - practice write

Invite students to share new sentences that give their readers the joy and satisfaction of figuring things out for themselves.

d) Ask young writers to look for adjectives such as *nice, fun, mean, pretty, cold, etc.,* in their own work. Ask them to listen in peer conferences for places one of their peer authors might have *Hit The Reader Over The Head.*

Show, Don't Tell is the advice frequently given to writers when they hit the reader over the head. This advice, however, often leads young writers to illustrate. They interpret it literally. To them, *show* means draw a picture and *tell* means write.

Alliteration

When children list words that all start with the same sound for phonics practice, they are using *alliteration*. Authors deliberately place two words starting with the same sound next to each other for the appealing sound it creates. Children's authors are particularly adept at this, deliberately using alliteration to make their writing sound melodic when read aloud.

Introduce your children to alliteration by immersing them in it. Read picture books that are heavy on alliteration. For example:

De Paola, Tomie. *Charlie Needs a Cloak*. New York: Simon and Chuster, 1973.
Dubanevich, Arlene. *Calico Cow*. New York: Viking, 1993.
Steig, William. *Sylvester and the Magic Pebble*. New York: Simon and Chuster 1969.
Steig, William. *The Toy Brother*. New York: HarperCollins, 1996.
Steig, William. *Roland, the Minstrel Pig*. New York: HarperCollins, 1968.

- Reread a book specifically to point out the alliteration after reading it for the content.
- Do oral work with alliteration: ask children to make up couplets of alliterative words. Remind them of the cartoon characters Mickey Mouse and Donald Duck. Tongue twisters are alliteration at work. *PeterPiper picked a peck of pickled peppers.* Rhyming is a variation of alliteration — using the same ending sound. *A silly cat, wore a hat.*
- Find the alliterative names of your students. Usually there are one or two children with an alliterative first and last name, or first and middle name. *Melanie Morris, Billy Bob Frazer.*
- Model alliteration in its most simple form: making up a name of a character in your writing: *My friend Mike Moran is a carpenter. He drives a truck. It says: Wood Worker on the side of the truck.*
- Invite students to try alliteration in their own writing.
- Model the skill several times. Call for its use as a target skill.

Your model: Alliteration use. Tab this page to find it quickly when you are ready to model alliteration in your personal writing.

Simile

Second-grade students can understand simile. (See Comparison, in Chapter 12.) Conduct a minilesson for second graders in the following fashion:

Show students a football. Suggest that they try to explain a football, by phone or in writing, to someone who has never seen one. The best way to do that would be to compare it to something the person might already know.

Model

Model a sentence that describes by comparison only. *The football is as large as a big loaf of bread.* Ask your students for other sentences that describe the football by comparing it to something almost everyone would know. Compare by color, size, shape, feel.

Practices Tamara

A foot ball is big as a loaf of bread.

It feels like a bumpy gulf ball.

A football is a color of a tree bank.

Its shaped like a egg.

Practicing

Invite students to bring in an object or find a picture of an object so they can try describing it by comparison only. Have them do the description first orally, in knee-to-knee peer conferences. Model such a conference with a student.

Your model: Decide on an object. Draw it in this text box to remind you. Make up several sentences using comparisons to describe the object. Tab this page to find it quickly when you present this model.

Sharing

Not all young writers' comparisons will take the standard simile form: as *woolly* as a *caterpillar*, or *shiny like plastic*. This is fine. Other forms of comparison children may use are: It is just like a_____, It's like a_____, It reminds me of_____, It's so _____that_____.

After the children have described their pictures or objects, ask them to share the comparisons, the similes, they heard. Write the children's comparisons on a chart. Invite young writers to add more to this chart as they hear them in peer conferences or they make them up themselves. (This provides another chance for young writers to get up and do something purposeful.)

Re-teach this lesson several times. Have students write one or two sentences using a simile. Then call for simile as a target skill in one of their ongoing personal writing pieces.

Your simile model: Write a few sentences of description and include a simile. Tab this page to find your model quickly.

Summary

Young children thrive on information. Support young writers' growth by teaching as many aspects of writing content as they can handle. Use their writing as a guide to determine which skills and techniques to model. Learn as much about the writing craft as you can, and learn to write with your students. Your writing community will prosper.

Section Four: Evaluation, Parent Education, Some Questions and Answers, Bibliography

Chapter 16
Evaluation

Efficient Record Keeping

In a well-established primary writing community, your students are in different parts of the writing process, are writing about different topics, are working on different target skills, and are at different stages of development. Therefore, they require different materials, lessons, and resources. Keeping track of this diversity is challenging. Keeping good records will help you organize writing sessions, plan lessons, and evaluate student progress. It will save your sanity

Sharing

In the primary grades, students range from early emergent to developing writers. They all must have the opportunity to develop a feeling of authorship and full membership in the writing community. You need to keep track of student participation in sharing components of the daily writing workshop. Select volunteers on a rotational basis and keep records of who has done what.

Keep a clipboard handy with a class list on it. Whenever you conduct an Author's Chair, model a peer conference, or use a student's manuscript in a lesson, check off the student names as they participate. Use the list to determine who needs an opportunity to share.

Where are Writers in the Writing Process

In first and second grade, some young writers will work on a piece of writing for several days. They may be working on a piece they are planning to publish, or that is part of the required work in the genre under study. They take their pieces through the entire writing process: prewriting; writing; a peer conference; revision; a teacher conference; editing; and publishing or readying for evaluation and portfolios. The final piece is accompanied by prewriting lists; drawings, or such; the draft, which contains compliments and, possibly, question stickers; evidence of editing; and the peer responders' initials.

To keep track of students' progress in the writing process, some teachers use a large wheel made from oaktag, divided into pie wedges that are labeled with the parts of

the process. Children move clothespins bearing their names from one wedge to another, around the rim of the wheel. The chart is large, and you can easily see what children need or what they should be doing. The young writers have a chance to get up and move about as they move their clothespins. They enjoy tracking their progress in this concrete fashion.

Other teachers draw a chart on the blackboard, using a column for each of the process stages. Young writers move a name tag across the board as they move from one writing process stage to another.

I prefer the wheel because there is no beginning and no end. Children do not race to reach the end as they might do with the linear version of the chart. The wheel also symbolizes the ongoing nature of writing work in the daily writing workshop.

Roving conference notes

You need to keep track of emergent writers' progress through the seven stages. You need to document their progress in the various target skills for lesson planning, parent conferences, and report cards.

A dated class list on a clipboard is handy for jotting down students' progress or diagnosing problems you note as you rove during the writing component of daily writing workshop. These notes do not need to be extensive. Here are sample entries made by a kindergarten teacher in a single session:

Name	Exhibited in Writin	Topic
Alex	wrapping text, more than one sentence	baby sister
David	reversing b's	brother
Casey	labeled three elements with correct consonants	fish store
Jason	copying word manatee from Ranger Rick	manatees
Carlos	needs help with finger spaces	counting
Fiona	starting writing on the right again	cats
Warren	asked me to write zamboni! in his word-bank	peewee hockey (He plays.)
Billy	holding pencil peculiarly	dog
Sarah	all capital letters, (sitting with Fiona)	cats

Self-evaluation

When young writers try to hand me a piece of writing and ask, *Is this good?* I do not take it. Instead, I ask them, *What do you think of it?* Or I say, *Tell me the part you think you did well*, or *Show me where you hit the target skill.*

If a target skill has been assigned, train young writers to ask, *What do you think of how I used target skill x? or Listen to my hook, or Listen to how I used 'later' and 'soon' instead of 'And then.'* Then your answer will be, *I hear how you used the target skill, and you did it very nicely. Good job.* Most children seek and respond to adult approval. Let your writers know what you are looking for in their writing, and praise that. You should be as specific as you can.

Encourage young writers to self-evaluate and satisfy themselves as well. This reinforces authorship and a sense of accomplishment (a legitimate source of self-esteem), and it keeps them engaged in their writing. When they base the selection of their best pieces on a reasonable set of criteria, it will help them see their progress as writers.

After several months of daily writing workshop with target-skill lessons, conferencing, and sharing, young writers will begin to appreciate what constitutes good writing at their grade level.

Criteria

Call young writers together with the goal of establishing criteria for them to evaluate their own writing. Tell them they will be looking through their body of writing and deciding which pieces to set aside in a portfolio of their best work.

Brainstorm with them about what constitutes good writing in their class. Many of the criteria they chose will reflect the target skills you have been teaching in a particular genre. Here are some criteria selected by primary-grade students. Some reflect emergent writers' opinions, and some reflect those of developing writers. Some of the criteria reflect writing-content skills, and some reflect writing-process procedures. Some are neither, but tell what children think good writing should be.

- It's got lots of action.
- It's funny. The other writers laughed when I read it.
- The picture is good.
- The picture is all colored in.
- It sounds good.
- It has finger spaces.
- It's about me.
- It's long.
- There is a period at the end.
- It has a title.
- My letters are good.
- I put my name on it.
- I used number words.
- I have a question hook.
- I started with a capital letter.
- I told lots of things about snakes.
- I used quotation marks.
- I told how I felt.
- I used big, fat, juicy verbs.
- I added more stuff about my cat.
- I used *soon* and *later*.

Work with young writers to come up with a reasonable number of criteria for them to use in selecting their best work. Encourage them to consider content and style as well as the cosmetic aspects of writing: punctuation, spelling and capitalization. These criteria are not written in stone; they will change as the writers progress. Publish the criteria on a classroom chart.

Selection of Best Work

Every three or four weeks, students should select their best work. Make arrangements for your writers to spread their work on the floor in a large area such as the gymnasium or a hall or on tables in the classroom. Remind them of the class criteria for good writing. Hang the chart in a conspicuous place.

Writers may ask other children for their opinions. This encourages them to feel they are a part of a community. They support and help each other with comments and compliments. Best work will be placed in their personal portfolios to show parents during conferences. Children will take the contents of the portfolio home at the end of the year.

Portfolio

After the children have selected the piece they will put in their portfolio, write on the board for them to copy: *I am putting this piece in my portfolio because...* Have them finish the sentence using criteria from the class list.

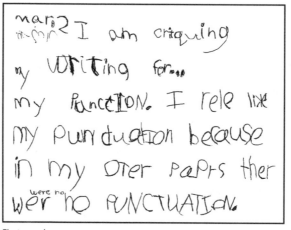

First grader

Writing Assessment

Writing assessment methods in the primary grades vary. For emergent writers, charting a child's progress through the writing-development stages is the most useful. For young developing writers, beyond Stages Six and Seven, assessing their writing for specific skill use works best. Whatever method you use, you must be able to verify progress, both for parents and for yourself.

Identifying the Emergent Stages

The best way to diagnose and document an emergent writer's progress is to look in her writing for the appearance of characteristic writing components of the successive stages. For the early-emergent writers, you can note what the writer *tells* you about her picture/writing.

Characteristic components, in order of increasing sophistication, are:
- drawing
- details in drawing
- letter labels
- strings of letters below the drawing or picture
- left-to-right directionality
- lists of repetitive letters/words/phrases
- sound-to-symbol relation
- initial consonant writing
- use of sight words
- use of end consonants
- use of vowels
- use of temporary spelling
- use of period
- consistency in using lower and upper case
- use of capital letters to start piece or sentence
- wrapping text correctly

Familiarize yourself with the various emergent-writing stages. Keep a writing-evaluation notebook with a page for each child. Record the date of the first evidence of a new stage, and note when you see consistent use of the associated components in her writing. Save a dated paper that demonstrates these components and place it in the child's portfolio. Add significant conference notes and anecdotes as well.

Hitting the Target

From children's practice writing, you can determine when they are able to hit the target, i.e., to use the target skill from a given lesson. Record when a child uses the target skill in his independent writing.

In first and second grade, call for children to submit a piece of writing to be assessed. They will choose the piece to be assessed for specific target-skill use. Give them time to revise their work. Assess their work only for the target skills you named. A writer who has demonstrated the correct use of the target skill gets top marks. You can reward outstanding work (great vocabulary, additional writing techniques, etc.) with bonus marks, gold stickers, or such.

A Scoring Rubric in Second Grade

During second grade, you can start to use a rubric that scores papers on elaboration, organization, focus (staying on topic), and conventions. Elaboration, independent of how well the information or details are arranged, should be given the most weight.

Second graders should start organizing their personal narratives chronologically. Their expository pieces should be organized with like-material clumped together or in successive sentences. At this grade level, it is appropriate to include beginnings and endings, in the form of a sentence, in your criteria for organization.

Score the writing only for the conventions that children can edit independently. Do not score papers for any skills you have not taught. Award bonus points for outstanding skill use.

Students using the rubric

In the latter half of second grade, show your young writers the scoring rubric, and teach them how to use it. Ask young writers to identify the criteria during Author's Chair, listening for elaboration, focus, chronological order, and time transitions in each other's narratives. They can also try this in peer conferences. Using the rubric and listening to each other's work for specific components of the rubric helps children become more aware of the quality of their own writing and what they need to do to improve it.

Chapter 17
Parent Education

To create an effective writing community, you need the understanding and cooperation of parents or guardians. Let them know about your writing program. Tell them about:

- daily writing workshop
- the ongoing nature of writing in your classroom
- target skills
- the function of temporary spelling
- class publishing and editing standards
- evaluation, assessment, and rubrics
- procedures requiring their help and understanding

Dear Parents

Write a letter to parents at the beginning of the school year. The following model includes a brief description of the writing process and how writing instruction will proceed in your classroom. Explain how they can help students prepare to write. Invite them to come in and observe the writing workshop.

Dear Parents,

Your children will be learning to write in our class. Not just learning to form letters and understanding that letters represent the sounds of our language, but learning to be authors. Here is what they will be doing and how you can help them.

- They will be selecting topics. You can help by asking them each morning: *What will you write about today?*
- They will be labeling their drawings and creating messages.
- They will be trying out writing techniques called target skills. You can help by asking them: *What is your target skill in this paper? What is your target skill this week?*
- They will be sharing their writing and asking their peers, *Is this clear? Is this interesting?* They will be revising by adding details.
- They will be editing their work independently for a few conventions. (Each marking period they will have more conventions to check. You will be informed what they are and can help your child with them.)
- They will be publishing some of their work.

When you see their work, you can help by talking to them about the **content**, what it is about. Here are some comments and questions that help a young author.

I like this...(picture, letter, label, word)
Did you tell all about the picture?
Can you tell me more about...?
What else do you know about this?
What will your next piece be about?

You, their audience and readers, will need to bear with them as they learn their craft. Receive their writing in the same spirit of encouragement that you do their music, art, and sports performances. That will help them become the best they can be.

Parent Night

Most schools schedule an evening for parents to meet teachers, visit their children's classrooms, and learn about the curriculum and school policies. Use part of your presentation time to explain your writing program. Use an overhead projector to show examples of student work, curriculum information, and assessment criteria. Display folders, notebooks, and hand-published books to support your explanation.

Make several videotapes of children working in your daily writing workshop to demonstrate the writing-process procedures they follow. Show the best tape to parents of the incoming class.

Parent Glossary

Parents will need to know the language of writing as well as terms in your writing program. Prepare a glossary for them and give it to them on Parent's Night or mail it with your initial letter. Include definitions of the new words. Some examples for the glossary are *prewriting, personal narrative, expository writing, peer conference, Author's Chair, compliment, target skill, focus, revision, editing, publishing.*

Writing Stays in School

Tell parents why they will not see writing coming home from school daily, that children need their writing on hand during workshop in order to practice revision and editing. Their children will bring writing home at the end of each marking period and at the end of the year. Make sure parents know they are invited to come in, by appointment or pre-arrangement, to see their child's folder of practice and ongoing pieces, and the writing portfolio.

Parent Involvement

Let parents know you welcome their help with class publishing projects by collecting pictures, taking photographs at events, typing children's work, and providing materials. Invite them to your class to hear Author's Chair. Organize a school-wide authoring celebration, and invite parents to attend.

Chapter 18
Some Questions and Answers

1. Should I write beneath children's writing so they and others can read it?

- Yes, when you are helping a student prepare for publishing a piece that will leave the classroom. You become the editor-in-chief of your class publishing firm.
- Yes, if the young writer is on the brink of breaking the sound-to-symbol code. Emergent writers in Stages Three and Four can use this help on request. Wean them from it as soon as possible.
- Yes, if a Stage-Five writer, who is beginning to read his own writing, needs to see the correct version of a word he has used but cannot decode.
- Yes, but not on every paper.
- Yes, if a student requests it.
- Not on papers of Stage One and Two writers, unless they request it.

2. Should I take dictation?

- Yes, for children in the first four stages. They need to see print principles modeled often. They need to hear their messages and see them converted to symbols.
- Yes, but do not do it for every child, in every writing session. Once a week is reasonable and practical.
- When you do, have children trace over the dictation and read it to peers.

3. Should I tell children how to spell words?

- Yes, but on a limited basis. Emphasize that they should phrase their request as: *How do I write the word...?*
- Encourage them, instead, to use environmental print, wall banks, other children, personal word lists, the Help Strip.
- Model the drafting strategy of using the first letter of the word, circling it and continuing.

The more strategies children have to find words, the less they will hound you for them.

4. Should I give topics or story starters to my primary students?

- An emphatic, NO! Young writers need to have control over the content of their pieces; they must know the subject well. When they do, they can concentrate on the mechanics of writing and composing skills and not be inhibited by the lack of knowledge or interest.
- Teach them how to use personal expertise and experiences as topic sources.
- Help them find topics from photographs, literature, and school activities.
- Be sure parents know their children will be writing every day. Encourage them to ask their child *What do you plan to write about today?*
- Remember, the emphasis in writing education, particularly in the early grades, is on target skills — writing techniques — not topics.

5. Should I assign writing?

- Yes, in second grade, you can and should assign (**not prompt**) writing to obtain samples for assessment/portfolios. Assign writing in a genre, assign the target skills, but let the children select topics from an array or use one of their own.
- Yes, you can assign writing after a theme study to find out what your students learned. Assess the content, not the writing, but note where further lessons and practice are indicated.

6. What are the children writing about day after day?

- They are writing about themselves. This may be stimulated by the literature (non-fiction and fiction) that you read to them.
- They are writing about things they are learning: science, geography, music, art, math.
- They are writing lists, informational pieces, opinions, picture responses, personal narratives, poems, invitations, notes to each other and you, plays, literature responses.

7. How do I get young writers to use webs and timelines?

- You don't. Primary writers are not ready for abstract graphic planners such as webs, clustering, mapping, timelines. Teach them to talk, draw, make lists, and look at pictures while they gather thoughts before writing.
- Teach first and second graders how to create and use lists linking and grouping things that go together.

8. How do I get young writers to write more elaborately?

- **Elaboration is directly proportional to the amount and quality of prewriting that an author does and the writer's depth of knowledge about the topic.** Provide the opportunity for your emergent writers to talk about their topics and to draw or cut and paste related pictures.
- Help them choose topics about which they know a great deal, usually based on their personal experience and expertise.
- Teach them elaborative techniques (see Chapters 12 and 15).
- Model elaborative writing.
- Use Author's Chair.
- Publish their work.

9. How do I get young writers to edit?

- Teach them to edit by ear.
- Have them edit for one convention at a time.
- Have them edit each other's papers.
- Set easy, independent editing standards for classroom publishing.
- Provide concrete aids for children to use, such as ink stamps and stickers, and clickers for editing by ear.

10. What about the children who cannot read their own writing?

- Reinforce letter formation using a variety of practices: water writing, wooden tracing patterns, large arm movement, blackboard work.
- Model finger spaces.
- Take some dictation from them. Have them trace this work for homework.
- When they can read, have them edit other children's papers.

11. What about the children who can't hear incomplete sentences or sentence endings?

- Invest time in choral-reading training using Big Books.
- Teach children to murmur-read and provide time for them to read with feeling with peers.
- Help children locate *who* and *what happened* in their writing.

12. What about children who write repetitively on one topic?

- No problem. Where would H. A. Rey have been if his editor told him to cut out the monkey stories? Or, what if Joanna Cole's editor told her that enough was enough with the yellow school-bus manuscripts? Repetitive topics are fine as long as the pieces are not the same and if new target skills are practiced in each piece. An assortment of topics does not guarantee writing progress.
- Make sure the writer works on a different target skill in each piece.
- Encourage writers who use a topic repetitively to write about it in different genres.

If a topic is not engaging, the young writer will eventually move on.

13. What about children who copy to publish but make new mistakes?

- Recognize that adult writers do this, too.
- Archive the first copy for proof of editing.
- Mask mistakes with labeling material or white correction fluid.
- Correct the new mistakes yourself.
- Get volunteers to type children's edited work for publication.
- Have second graders underline, in a bright color, the edits they made on the first drafts. These will be more conspicuous when they copy for publishing.

14. What about over-dependent writers who need assurance at every turn?

- Team them up with competent and helpful types as writing partners.
- Remodel What-to-Do-When-the-Teacher-is-Busy and How-to-Get-Help.
- Encourage young writers to work on short pieces until their confidence level is higher.

These are just a few representative questions posed by teachers who are building writing communities in the primary grades. You will have more. Read other professional books and journal articles about teaching children to write. Find colleagues who are working toward the same goal as you. Share best practices.

Most important of all, take that huge step: Teach the content of writing. Believe your young students can and will learn to write. I promise they will not let you down.

Bibliography

Ackerman, Diane. *A Natural History of the Senses*. New York: Random House, 1990.

Freeman, Marcia. *Building a Writing Community*. Gainesville, FL: Maupin House Publishing, 1995.

Cambourne, Brian and Turbill, Jan. *Coping With Chaos*. Australia: Primary English Teaching Assoc., 1987.

Parkes, Brenda. *Discovery Link series*. New York: Newbridge Communications, Inc., 1998.

Schwartz, Linda. *I Love Lists*. Santa Barbara, CA: The Learning Works, 1988.

Alphabet Training Letters

Lakeshore Learning Materials, 2695 E. Dominguez St., P. O. Box 6261, Carson, CA 90749

1997 Catalogue: page 138, Language: learning the alphabet: Motor Letter System: lower and upper case manuscript (printing) wooden patterns with large knobs for child to trace the pattern of a letter.

Children's Books About The Writing Craft

Asher, Sandy. *Where Do You Get Your Ideas*. New York: Walker and Company, 1987.

Bauer, Marian Dane. *What's Your Story; A Young Person's Guide to Writing Fiction*. New York: Clarion Books, 1992.

Benjamin, Carol Lee. *Writing for Kids*. New York: Thomas Y. Crowell, 1985.

Dubrovin, Vivian. *Write Your Own Story*. New York: Franklin Watts, 1984.

Kinghorn, Harriet R. and Peltor, Mary Helen. *Every Child a Storyteller*. Englewood, CO: Teacher Ideas Press, 1991.

Greenfield, Howard. *Books: From Writer To Reader*. New York: Crown Publishers, Inc., 1989.

Peck, Robert Newton. *The Secrets of Successful Fiction*. Cincinnati, OH: Writers' Digest Books, 1980.

Tchudi, Susan and Stephen. *The Young Writer's Handbook*. New York: Aladdin Books, Macmillan Publishing Co., 1984.

Appendix

Second-grade teachers should expect most students, by the end of the year, to:

- use lower-case letters consistently, reserving upper-case for the conventions of capitalization
- write in complete sentences, including compound sentences and expanded sentences (phrases that tell where, and when)
- chose a topic independently
- write several paragraphs on a topic
- organize expository writing using list/linking, physical sorting
- organize narratives chronologically, using time orienters where appropriate
- use a variety of hooks (onomatopoeia, question, exclamation, setting) in a one or two sentence introduction
- compose endings of one or two sentences that tell how they fell about the topic or event, or using a universal word (all, always, everyone, everybody, every time, etc.)
- share their writing with a peer and identify target-skill use in a peer's writing
- know how to compliment and ask questions of peer writers
- revise by adding words and sentences
- revise by substituting words: time orienters, pronouns for nouns and vice versa, strong verbs for ordinary, specific nouns for general nouns
- use a variety of attributes and comparisons in descriptive writing
- edit each other's for: end punctuation, capitalization (I, names, start of paragraph), content words, common sight words, and Dolch Primary words.
- select best work for their portfolios based on personal or class criteria
- hand-publish several pieces